WHAT STUDENTS SAY ABOUT THIS BOOK:

“Extraordinary book to which all students can relate. The author did a fantastic job of connecting with readers to empower them to do better in their own lives. The five-minute ‘to-do’ list and 45 techniques are extremely useful and will not only help you in college, but also in real life.”

Marquis Gaubatz, Sophomore, Public Relations, University of Texas, San Antonio

“This helpful and humorous collection of tips can foster the perpetually busy student’s success in and outside the classroom. The book is a quick read, yet packs in the necessary information. The candor and wit are refreshing.”

Sophia Mossberg, Freshman, English/American Literature, Barnard College, Columbia University, NY

“I tried out Berk’s ‘to-do’ list and found it very useful. Instead of feeling overwhelmed, I felt more relaxed and better able to take on any busy day. The prioritizing also helped greatly. I figured out what I needed to get done first and what could be put off to a later time. I would definitely recommend this book to college students, especially incoming freshman. Maybe that first year won’t feel so overwhelming to them.”

Erin Durisin, Senior, History, Lycoming College, PA

“The five-minute plan is very useful and can make or break students’ time management abilities, especially if they have no prior experience. The techniques mentioned in the book are relevant to both undergraduate as well as graduate students.”

Matthew Evins, Graduate Student, Instructional Design and Technology, Miami University, OH

“I highly recommend that ALL college students read this book. The five-minute ‘to-do’ list is a must! These techniques will reduce your stress, improve your grades, and provide a foundation for your continued success in every area throughout your lifetime.”

Elizabeth Geringer, Senior, Psychology, California State University, Channel Islands

“Without these time-management techniques
scratching our heads thinking about what nee

ally getting things done. This book is not only hysterical, it keeps your interest piqued, and most important, the techniques are effective!"

Yaffa Ross, Junior, Criminal Justice, University of Texas, San Antonio

"This book really helps outline both the importance of getting everything done, but still finding time to engage in social activities and stay healthy. Even though I already have my own techniques, the five-minute 'to-do' list helped me figure out even more efficient ways to plan and organize my time."

Megan Bullick, Freshman, Creative Writing/Music, Lycoming College, PA

"Manage the time to read this book, and you will find time to manage your life. This book is an excellent stepping-stone to helping college students discover new techniques in their time-management personality. A great inspiration to developing a healthy college lifestyle."

Allison Corbin, Junior, Instrumental Music Education, Miami University, OH

"Every college student should pick up this book and read it. The 'to-do' list is very useful and your best guide to daily planning when you're in school as well as when you're out."

Janae Brooks, Freshman, Nursing, Youngstown State University, OH

"I took pleasure in reading the book and feel that I have taken away some time-management skills that I wouldn't have otherwise. All 45 techniques are useful. I would definitely recommend this book to other students. It challenges you to implement the techniques and see how useful they can be."

Scott Reed, Junior, English Literature (Secondary Education), Lycoming College, PA

The Five-Minute Time Manager for College Students

Other Books by Ron Berk

Professors Are from Mars®, Students Are from Snickers®

Humor as an Instructional Defibrillator

Top Secret Tips for Successful Humor in the Workplace

Thirteen Strategies for Measuring College Teaching

The 7 Habits of Highly Infected People

The 8th Habit: From Infection to Sick Leave

The One-Minute Meeting

Chunky Soup for the Soul

Leadership on the Fly: Principles of Jack Bauer

Who Moved My Lox and Cream Cheese?

The North-South-East-West Beach Diet

Tuesdays with Dr. Phil

The Greed-Driven Life

THE FIVE-MINUTE TIME MANAGER FOR COLLEGE STUDENTS

How to Turbo-Charge Your Academic and Personal Productivity

RONALD A. BERK

Forewords by
MEGAN BULLICK, MATTHEW EVINS, and
ELIZABETH GERINGER

Coventry Press

www.coventrypress.com

Published by Coventry Press (www.coventrypress.com)

13-digit ISBN: 978-0-9823871-1-5

Library of Congress Control Number: 2009906796

Printed in the United States of America

First Edition, 2009

Special discounts are available on quantity purchases.

To My Students
Past, Present, and Future

Who teach me, entertain me, energize me,
and give my life meaning

Contents

Acknowledgments

WRITING A BOOK ON TIME MANAGEMENT TAKES AN INORDINATE amount of time. If you only knew. Taking some of my own medicine and applying the techniques described herein were absolutely critical to the completion of this book. Few writers have the luxury of giant blocks of uninterrupted time. I'm certainly not one of those few. Aside from doing the essential research and reading nearly every major work on the topic, I wrote pieces of the book while sitting in traffic, airports, airplanes, hotel lobbies, coffee shops, doctors' offices, the Broadway show *Spamalot*, and the Radio City Rockettes Christmas Spectacular®. I compiled most of the list of travel destinations for technique #25 while standing in line for almost an hour for Passport Control in Dubai International Airport at 1 A.M. Writing everywhere you can, including in the comfort of your own office in your underwear, is the most time effective and efficient approach to producing books. These same strategies apply to your studying. They can significantly increase your academic and personal productivity. Give it a whirl.

The task of taking my content and transforming it into a "quick read" book for students like you required the support of a publication team of editors, designers, and typographers. The head of that team is *Judy Coughlin*, Production Manager and "Editor Par Excellence." I am indebted to her for waving her magic wand over the original manuscript to create the polished product you're now holding. Her meticulous attention to every detail in the publication process is evident in that product. I also want to thank my super-creative cover designer *Kathleen Dyson* for applying her gifts to my book titles.

Despite the efforts of several professionals in the production of this book, there is always the possibility of substantive and editorial errores or omis sions. None of these people is responsible. Ultimately, there is only one person who should be held totally accountable for the mistakes in this book, and that person, of course, is Stephen Colbert.

The acid test for whether the material between these covers is of any value was the feedback from real, live, warm-bodied, sleep-deprived, overworked, party-loving students from colleges and universities throughout the United States. I contacted several faculty colleagues and asked them to identify one or more students who would be willing to review the book. I want to express my gratitude to those colleagues for their assistance: *Karen Becker, Ann Eisenberg, Steven Fleischer, Darby Lewes, Barbara Millis, Barbara Mossberg, Ed Nuhfer,* and *Michael Theall.*

However, I especially want to acknowledge the contributions of this diverse group of 10 students: *Janae Brooks, Megan Bullick, Allison Corbin, Erin Durisin, Matthew Evins, Marquis Gaubatz, Elizabeth Geringer, Sophia Mossberg, Scott Reid,* and *Yaffa Ross.* I thank them for their time and valuable comments on the usefulness of the five-minute plan and the 45 techniques. All of their thoughtful comments were incorporated into the content in some form. In addition, three of those students—*Megan Bullick, Matthew Evins,* and *Elizabeth Geringer*—wrote forewords for the book. I am grateful to them for greatly enhancing the credibility of my work.

Finally, I thank my family—my wife *Marion*, for her patience, encouragement, and strategy #45; my incredible daughters, *Boo Boo* (a.k.a. Marissa), who helped design flyers and brochures to market this book, and *Cori* (a.k.a. Corinne), whose blogs keep me informed and entertained; my FAVE son-in-law *Chris*, for his supportiveness in all of my endeavors; my playful and hilarious granddaughter *Ella*; and my *Mommy* who at 90 years old is still sharp and serves as the linchpin for this family. They all provide me with endless sources of joy, laughter, and inspiration. Without them, this book would be meaningless.

Forewords

THE TRANSITION FROM HIGH SCHOOL TO COLLEGE CAN BE difficult in many ways, but perhaps the hardest obstacle to overcome is learning how to manage time wisely. With so many new, interesting professors and students to meet, even the most organized and structured student has difficulty remembering all of the homework assignments due tomorrow, the musical instrument that hasn't been practiced in a week, or the untouched basketball gathering dust underneath the bed.

Ron Berk's five-minute "to-do" list and the 45 time-management techniques help explain how you can efficiently finish everything that you need to accomplish and still have time for the activities that you want to do. The book also abounds with helpful hints on not only how to maximize your time, but also how to feel great and energized every day. His conversational style, rich with humor and wit, helps make a normally mundane and tedious subject entertaining and stimulating. *The Five-Minute Time Manager* is a great read for all college students, no matter what their level of expertise or experience.

Megan Bullick
Freshman, Creative Writing/Music
Lycoming College, PA

In the mid-1990s, I read Stephen Covey's *The 7 Habits of Highly Effective People.* It made me consider various ways I could be successful in everything that I do. The problem was that I was reading a book designed for managers and employees who work in the corporate world. At that time, I was just entering high school, so the book was way over my head. I noticed that several of the strategies recommended in the book didn't apply to me and probably wouldn't for many years to come. It was difficult to relate to a lot of the material.

Now that I have graduated from college, I feel that I've developed time-management skills that will last a lifetime. After reading Ron Berk's book, I reflected on the time it took for me to decipher and convert Covey's content into a language I could understand. Had Berk's book or another written for college students been available when I was an undergraduate, it would have changed the way I organized and planned my life.

One activity that I never enjoyed (and still don't) is reading. I always felt that there were more important things that I could be doing with my time than reading a book about how to do something that I was already doing. This feeling comes from years of maintaining good time-management skills. There was always a project or term paper to engage my time. I thought it was counterproductive and a waste of time to read a book on time management when I was constantly trying to keep up with my class assignments. It could throw off *MY* time-management schedule.

However, that feeling changed once I committed to reading this book. I couldn't put it down. The language, concepts, and flow of the book made it possible to finish in 90 minutes. Not only do the strategies described make complete sense from start to finish, but it also provides a quick refresher on any one or more strategies if you need it.

However, the most significant characteristic of this book that makes it so easy to read is the *humor*. This book is hysterical! From the introduction (which I usually skip, but I highly recommend you read) to strategy #45, you will encounter humor everywhere. One of Ron's most memorable traits is his uncanny ability to make you laugh in print or in person; it's almost like he has a second language—"humorese." If you've ever had the privilege of hearing one of his presentations, then you know that a heavy dose of humor goes a long way to liven up dry material.

This book is the perfect prescription for anyone looking to get his or her life on track by setting appropriate priorities and planning a college schedule accordingly. If you are looking for a quick sample before you commit to reading the entire book, I strongly encourage you to check out the following five tips: *Schedule Time for Social Activities* (#9), *Review Your Plans Frequently and Make Adjustments as Necessary* (#12), *Try to Stay 1 to 3 Days Ahead in Your Assignments* (#20), *Eliminate Distractions* (#26), and *Be Punctual* (#37).

Among all of the excellent tips and tricks in this book, those are the five that would have changed the way I managed my life over the years. Even now that I work full time while pursuing a master's degree and after having read this book, I have made adjustments in the planning and organization of my time that would never have occurred to me otherwise. Whether you're an undergraduate or graduate student thinking about whether to read this book, I have just one piece of advice: "*JUST READ IT!*" It can change the way you do everything in college and beyond.

Matthew Evins
Graduate Student, Instructional Design & Technology
Miami University, OH

The life of a typical college student is driven by what has to be accomplished by the end of each day. At universities around the world students are wondering, "How am I going to find the time to get it all done today?" Pressure to succeed in an incredibly competitive academic world is just one piece of the puzzle for today's college student. Many students are on their own for the first time in their lives. They are beginning to learn how to manage finances, keep up on their health, feed themselves, wash clothes, and strengthen relationships. In addition, students must find enough hours in the day to keep up with the demands of many higher level college courses. There is only *one way to survive college* with pride in your accomplishments, lifelong knowledge, and goals for your future—MANAGE YOUR TIME!

Ron Berk's book is an excellent source for any college student. The five-minute "to-do" list is a must! It is the first step to gain control over a hectic college schedule. This easy tool quickly becomes a habit and relieves the pressure to remember excessive amounts of detailed information. By making this a regular morning routine, you will not waste time trying to remember what you have to get accomplished that day.

The book is organized in a straightforward manner; it's easy to mark and find the techniques that are particularly useful for rereading. There is no need to use all the techniques at once. The book is designed so that the techniques build on each other. As you adopt and become competent with one technique, you will naturally begin to acquire skills in another technique without even realizing it.

After quickly and thoroughly reading the entire book in less than two hours, certain topics piqued my interest. Since then, I have read these sections several times in order to master them as I work on trying to make my daily routine uncomplicated. You will be able to take away key points that will ultimately change the way you tackle and successfully manage the stress of college life.

One additional benefit to reading this book is the humor. Successful college students who want to improve their time management are serious about their goals. But this book is amusing and entertaining. The writer takes serious issues that affect the health and future of every college student and converts them into entertaining reading.

I highly recommend that ALL college students read this book. By making a little bit of effort to learn the techniques in this book, you will soon realize that you really do have extra time. No more cramming, no more missed assignments, and no more sleepless nights stressing over the research papers that still need to get done. Applying these techniques as a college student will reduce your stress, improve your grades, and provide a foundation for your continued success in every area throughout your lifetime.

Elizabeth Geringer
Senior, Psychology
California State University, Channel Islands

Introduction

As the signature song from the smash-hit, Tony-Award winning Broadway musical *Rent* says:

Five Hundred Twenty-Five Thousand
Six Hundred Minutes
Five Hundred Twenty-Five Thousand
Moments So Dear
Five Hundred Twenty-Five Thousand
Six Hundred Minutes
How Do You Measure, Measure a Year?
In Daylight, in Sunsets
In Midnights, in Cups of Coffee
In Inches, in Miles
In Laughter, in Strife
In Five Hundred Twenty-Five Thousand
Six Hundred Minutes
How Do You Measure a Year in the Life?

"Seasons of Love" challenges you to think about how you measure *your* time and how *you* use it. Ultimately, your time is defined by what you deem important, which is reflected in *your* goals, values, and priorities.

It's All About *YOUR* Time!

In college you have certain requirements that take blocks of time from your total available time. If you spend 15 to 18 hours a week in class and 30 to 45 hours in course-related activities, such as reading, studying for tests, writing papers, and eating pizza, those hours translate into 40,500–56,700 minutes per semester. That's a lot of time.

How does this time relate to your lifestyle? According to recent national surveys, college students exercise infrequently, drink too much, do not get enough sleep, cram for exams by studying all night, take controlled substances, and eat the wrong foods. Their parents are probably asking: "Where did we go right?"

An effective time manager cannot live that type of fun, hedonistic lifestyle, at least not yet. Something has to change. Your courses, assignments, and personal activities will guide you through the day, week, and month. Your focus will be on academic performance, not on the aforementioned abusive activities.

Although your class time is nonnegotiable, your course-related activities are negotiable. *Suppose you could knock the activities time down by 20%, or 5,400–8,100 minutes per semester.* Does that interest you? What would you do with all of that time? "Not a problem, dude." Doing one simple planning activity that takes five minutes a day could free up that time. If you want to know how to execute that plan, keep reading.

When I ask college students to raise their hands if they've taken a time-management workshop or course, usually about 10% put their hands up. The reason: The remaining 90% report that either they don't have the time for or access to such a course. Well that time has come, and it's NOW. The best part of this book is that whatever you choose to read and incorporate into your daily routine can only help you become a better time manager. *You have nothing to lose and lots of time to gain.* That's a pretty good deal.

Benefits of Effective Time Management

So what is *time management*? It is simply about making choices about how you spend your time. Over the past 35 years, a variety of techniques and tools have been developed and tested to help workers more effectively plan and schedule their time to increase productivity. Although the techniques were originally intended for the business community and professionals in different occupations, they were later extended to personal life tasks. Everybody could use many of the techniques to improve their daily time management.

Why bother to take the time to learn how to be an effective time manager? What's in it for you besides time? Actually "time" is a worthy benefit by itself. Consider the following scenario: You have efficiently used time to complete *what you HAVE to do*, such as coursework, laundry, and student government meetings. As a result, guess what? There's still more laundry to do. NO, but you now have a sizable amount of time left over to do *what you WANT to do*, such as party, play with your significant other, rehearse for a play/musical, and finish the laundry. *Bottom line*: You have the best of both worlds, plus you'll get a lot of laundry washed. You also have balance in your life between college work and laundry, I mean play.

If those perks aren't sufficiently compelling, several studies have found the following *10 personal benefits*. Effective time management

- Provides a sense of empowerment
- Increases your self-esteem and confidence
- Decreases your stress, tension, and anxiety
- Reduces your frustration
- Increases your energy level
- Provides a sense of accomplishment
- Gives you a feeling of satisfaction and achievement

- Increases your productivity
- Fosters the release of your creativity and imagination
- Permits you to eat better in a relaxed mode

Imagine the *feeling of being ahead, relaxed, and in control with buckets of free time to squander or to pursue what you want to do.* That's what makes dreams and spring break vacations in your parents' timeshare in Cancun possible. Alternatively, consider *being behind, unprepared, pressured, and playing catch-up all of the time with the accompanying stress, tension, and frustration*—you never have enough time, you feel overwhelmed, and you are constantly rushed, with little or no time for yourself or anybody else. That's what makes nightmares and Freddy Krueger possible.

Which of the preceding descriptions comes closest to characterizing you now? Certainly controlled substances can help with the latter, but you won't be able to function. If you want to experience the dreamlike feel of the former, peruse the next few paragraphs.

Get to the Point—Don't Waste My Time!

As a full-time or part-time college student, you probably don't have much time to fool around. My motto for this book is: *Get to the Point—Don't Waste My Time!* It could be the mantra for time-management practitioners. Our time is valuable, and neither of us has the luxury of wasting it.

There are nearly 50 books in print on time management written by the biggest names in business, such as Stephen Covey, Dan Kennedy, Alec Mackenzie, Brian Tracey, Alan Lakein, David Allen, and Richard Walsh. However, their books and those of other authors on the topic are intended for CEOs and top executives (*Sentenceus Interruptus:* Excuse me, but these are the executives who make us mad because they take extravagant junkets on their private jets to the French Riviera, Dubai, or Tahiti at our expense), other business leaders, corporate personnel, entrepreneurs, idiots, and dummies, but NOT college students, especially freshman who might benefit most from that information. You don't even have the time to read those books.

Otherwise, there are usually chapters in student success and study skills books related to time management; newsletters; and several lists of online time-management tips for students. That pretty much covers the resources currently available to students.

Based on all of these sources, I created an inventory of the most effective time-management techniques intended for employees in business and industry and the tips recommended for college students from the various sources. Redundancies were eliminated and a final list was compiled that represented evidence-based techniques and "best practices" that could be applied to the academic and personal lives of college students.

A Five-Minute Plan, Plus 45 Other Techniques

What can this book tell you in short order about time management that you don't already know? Many of you may have read Stephen Covey's *The 7 Habits of Highly Effective People,* which describes a few very useful techniques; others may have read zip. Among the wide range of techniques that experts on this topic recommend, I have extracted and adapted 46 that are a "best fit" for your time demands . . . WAIT, STOP SCREAMING!! You don't have to read all 46. I don't even remember where I left off when you started your tirade. Oh, and one technique in particular can guide your college life every day but will require only five minutes of your day. Seeeee. You can just do that one and save time. Those five minutes may occur the night before or the morning of the day being planned.

If you make that plan and commit to following it every day, you will be able to increase your efficiency in tackling course requirements and other daily tasks by 20% or more. That means *you could gain six to nine hours per week to engage in other academic or nonacademic activities*, such as hang gliding, bungee jumping, NASCAR racing, bull fighting, hot-dog-eating contests, and the like. Your success in this time-management strategy will depend on your level of commitment and strength. Anyone can do it. The strategy is easy; the commitment is tough.

The package of 46 techniques consists of a detailed description of the five-minute plan, plus brief accounts with examples of 45 other techniques. The first 12 will help you sharpen your daily plans. The next 24 time-saving strategies relate to studying. The final 9 are general time savers and rules for all students. Every one of the 45 techniques will save you time and increase your daily efficiency. As noted previously, they have been gleaned from the most authoritative sources on the topic. (*Note:* I've become a very thorough gleaner.) *Pick any technique that catches your eyeballs as you skim the Contents. Read it, internalize it, and adopt it as your own.* The more techniques you can incorporate into your daily thoughts and actions, the more effective and efficient a time manager you will become. Eventually, you may end up with so much time on your hands that you could use it to help others or go snowboarding.

1

The Five-Minute "To-Do" List

MUCH OF YOUR TIME RIGHT NOW IS DOMINATED BY YOUR professors' requirements. Fortunately or unfortunately, they change every semester. So once you think you've figured out what one professor wants and you receive an *A*, you discover that the section of another course she teaches in the spring is already full and you have to take a different section with another "unknown" professor. This course selection and scheduling process goes on semester after semester for the rest of your life.

The syllabi for your courses represent your blueprints for course success. The readings, tests, term papers, projects, and other assignments are your primary tasks for the semester. The trick is how to keep up with all of that work and get a high grade without ruining your life as you now know it. This is where time-management strategies can help you accomplish the former and minimize the ruining part.

Why Do You Need a List?

You need to create a list. Not just yet, though. This *list* requires that you write down all of your activities in a calendar format for easy access daily, weekly, and monthly. (*Sidebar:* I wish I could take credit for this technique, but it was actually recommended 35 years ago by Alan Lakein in his groundbreaking *Time Management: How to Get Control of Your Time and Your Life* and popularized by Stephen Covey in his *The 7 Habits of Highly Effective People.* We now jump to the next paragraph because this sidebar was so long.)

I know what you're thinking: "Why do I have to write down my classes and activities? I have a good memory." Not that good. You simply cannot keep a mental list of all your activities and appointments without forgetting something. Those activities will also increase each year. Cramming that stuff into your brain will eventually fill all of your RAM and, one day, when you least expect it, it will explode all over your room. EWWW!

Daily Planners

For many years, business leaders and employees used paper day planners and organizers available from a variety of companies, such as Day Runner, Day Timer, Filofax, Franklin Covey®, and Planner Pad. These days, tech savvy college students like you prefer a PDA, iPhone, or PC/Mac to create their schedules.

The PDA provides a wide array of features and capabilities, including Web accessibility, games, phone service, microwaving, and coffee making. Check *Consumer Reports* for reviews of the latest models, features, and prices for the electronic day-timer that best fits your needs. The iPhone and many other phones contain the essential PDA capabilities. All PDAs have rechargeable batteries, so make sure yours is recharged regularly and synchronized with your PC to back up your schedule and directories. Take it with you wherever you go, and keep it up to date. A hard metal protective cover is also advisable to protect its delicate little innards from the usual abuse, fire, bullets, and radiation.

"To-Do" List Software

In addition to PDAs or iPhones, there are specific software programs for your PC that you can use to document your "to-do" list. They also provide a variety of other time-management features that will fit anyone's specific needs. Three of the more popular programs are Achieve Planner (Effexis Software), Calendar Creator (Encore Software), and TreePad (Freebyte). Achieve Planner is the most comprehensive time-management system available; Calendar Creator provides templates of daily, weekly, monthly, and yearly planners with Franklin Covey® layouts; TreePad is a personal information manager, organizer, database, and word processor. A free 30-day trial period is available to test these software packages. Achieve Planner, in particular, is amazing.

Create the "To-Do" List

Now it's time. Get ready. Isn't this exciting? If you enter the information described in the following steps into your PDA or PC calendar, you will be on your way to becoming an effective time manager. These are the steps you need to take to create your daily five-minute "to-do" list.

Step 1: List Your Tasks and Activities

List the tasks and activities you need to accomplish in today's date in half-hour and one-hour blocks, if possible. Include all course activities and personal errands. For example:

6:30	Prayer, devotions, or quiet time
7:00	Breakfast
7:30	Check e-mails/TMs
8:00	Econ. class
9:00	Econ.—Hi-lite Chaps. 6–7
10:00	Chem.—Rev. for quiz
11:00	Chem. class
12:00	Lunch/Check e-mails/TMs
1:00	Doctor
2:15	Fencing practice
3:00	Meet Laticia at coffee bar
3:30	Bank deposit
4:00	Stat. class
5:00	Stat.—do probs. 1–3
5:30	Psych—Rev. Chap. 2 for quiz
6:00	Jog 3 miles
6:45	Dinner
7:00	Econ.—outline section one of paper
8:00	Watch *NCIS*
9:00	Stat.—finish probs. 3–6
10:00	Check e-mails/TMs/phone messages; Watch *L & O: SVU*

Step 2: Determine the Importance and Urgency of Your Activities

Determine the importance and urgency of each activity. Your daily activities can be lumped into six major categories:

1. ***A-priority non-negotiable classes and tests*** dominate much of your schedule. They are *important and urgent*. You should make every effort to attend your classes no matter how boring they are.
2. ***A-B-C priority negotiable class assignments*** are *important*, but may be *urgent* or *not urgent.* Same-day or next-day readings, problems, and lab work are urgent **A**s. Studying for quizzes is urgent; preparing for quarterly, midterm, or final exams should be semi-urgent (**B**) and then urgent (**A**) as the test day approaches. Term papers and projects due at midterm and at end of term are **C**s. If they're planned properly, they shouldn't become **A**s or **B**s.
3. ***Personal tasks***, such as trips to the bank, grocery store, Laundromat, cleaners, post office, and coffee shop, have more flexibility. They are **B**s or **C**s, which are *important and not urgent*, unless you really need that cup of Joe first thing in the morning. Car repair and some of those trips that have been left to the last minute can be **A**s. Cleaning your room, desk, or apartment and shopping at Bergdorf-Goodman, Neiman Marcus, and Hugo Boss also fit this category.
4. ***Relationships*** with friends, family, classmates, and significant others require commitment. Activities with them in restaurants, bars, parties, and dates involve time during the week (**A**s and **B**s), on weekends (**B**s and **C**s), and during holidays (**C**s). They are *important and urgent* and *not urgent.*
5. ***Entertainment activities***, including concerts, movies, theater, TV, video games, and sports events, fit in between the **A**s and **B**s during the week and **B**s and **C**s on the weekend. They are *important* to you and may be *urgent* or *not urgent.*
6. ***Electronic communications***, including e-mail, text messaging, Facebook, LinkedIn, MySpace, Twitter, and phone calls, can be time eaters. The subject matter of the communication

determines whether it is *important and urgent* or *unimportant and not urgent*. Course-related messages are **A**s or **B**s; social contacts are **C.**

Step 3: Assign Priorities to Your Activities

Assign a priority to each activity based on its importance and urgency, as follows:

A = high priority, important and urgent, must be completed that day
B = medium priority, important and slightly less urgent, desirable to complete that day after **A**s are completed
C = low priority, "nice to do" activities, not essential that day, can be deferred to another day

6:30	Prayer, devotions, or quiet time **A**
7:00	Breakfast **A**
7:30	Check e-mails/TMs **A–C**
8:00	Econ. class **A**
9:00	Econ.—Hi-lite Chaps. 6–7 **B**
10:00	Chem.—Rev. for quiz **A**
11:00	Chem. class **A**
12:00	Lunch/Check e-mails/TMs **A–C**
1:00	Doctor **A**
2:15	Fencing practice **A**
3:00	Meet Laticia at coffee bar **C**
3:30	Bank deposit **B**
4:00	Stat. class **A**
5:00	Stat.—do probs. 1–3 **A**
5:30	Psych—Rev. Chap. 2 for quiz **B**
6:00	Jog 3 miles **A**

6:45 Dinner **A**
7:00 Econ.—outline section one of paper **C**
8:00 Watch *NCIS* **B**
9:00 Stat.—finish probs. 3–6 **A**
10:00 Check e-mails/TMs/phone messages; Watch *L & O: SVU* **A/B**

Notice that activities that are part of your daily routine and required become automatic **A**s. Those include your devotions, meals, classes, and exercise. Every day they would be on your list. So what tasks are optional? Course assignments may be **A**, **B**, or **C**, depending on due date. Reading preparation for next class is usually **A** or **B**. Tests are **A** or **B**. Term papers and projects are typically **B** or **C**.

Step 4: Analyze Your Activities Matrix

Let's summarize the preceding activities and those in all six categories in the form of a 2 × 2 matrix developed originally by Stephen Covey to classify workplace activities as Important–Not Important and Urgent–Not Urgent. Figure 1 is an adaptation of his model to college student activities.

Use this matrix to visualize where your activities fit in terms of importance and urgency. At least *90% of your activities are important.* Of those, *35% are urgent and 55% not urgent.* Only a paltry 10% of the activities, mostly social communications and entertainment, are *unimportant and urgent* or *not urgent.*

Based on that distribution, you might want to adjust your priorities. With all of the important activities, scrutinize those in the urgent quadrant to determine whether any can be shifted over to the not urgent quadrant. For example, try not to leave assignments until the last minute; instead, do them as soon as possible so you

Figure 1. Time-Management Matrix for College Activities

	Urgent	Not Urgent
Important	All classes Taking quizzes and tests Same day or next day readings, problems, and lab assignments Prayer, devotions, or quiet time Same day medical/dental appointments Some e-mails/phone calls/TMs Family and other relationships Exercise Car repair Coffee Meals	Long-term assignments • Term papers • Projects Future readings, problems, and lab assignments Studying for quizzes and tests Meetings/rehearsals Some relationships Some meals and snacks Entertainment/sports events Personal tasks • Bill paying • Bank transactions • Post office mailings • Future medical/dental appointments • General car maintenance • Grocery shopping • Washing/ironing clothes • Clothes shopping • Cleaning room
Not Important	Some e-mails/TMs/phone calls Some requests by friends, family, etc.	Social e-mails/TMs/phone calls Excessive entertainment Excessive PC activities Excessive cleaning (Kidding!)

have a two-day or longer jump on readings. That way you need only review the chapters or notes on the chapters before class. Also, reduce the length of your social conversations until you have more free time. Tell your mother you'll be back in touch with her later in the week. She can handle it, but be gentle.

Just listing your activities and adhering to your daily schedule will increase your free time. Despite the number of activities in your preceding "to-do" list, there are gaps of time between those activities that can be used. Of course, there are also techniques to improve your time distribution that will increase your efficiency in completing your current activities. The remainder of the book is devoted to these techniques.

BERK'S BOTTOM LINE: Obviously, the four steps described in this section cannot be completed in five minutes. They will require six. Kidding. A little TM humor. Set up your daily schedule in your PDA for the first week of classes or whenever you begin. *Plug in your routine activities and class schedule first; then add all of the other activities daily.* That can be done the night before or the morning of the day of the "to-do" list. Don't forget to recharge your PDA overnight. Listing the assignments and personal tasks, plus assigning the **A**s, **B**s, and **C**s to all entries should take five minutes. It will be the most important and urgent five minutes of your day. After the first couple of weeks, the *prioritized "to-do" list* will be part of your daily routine.

The next challenge is to adhere to that list and tackle one **A** at a time, then each **B**, and possibly a **C** or two. As you become more efficient at time management, you will be finishing more and more activities per day. You'll wonder how the extra time popped up. Surprise, surprise! You'll be amazed at your own growth as an effective time manager.

2

Sharpen Your Planning Schedule

1. Identify Your Values

Do you have any values? Of course you do. Maybe you just haven't thought about them recently. Well, guess what? "This paragraph is ending." Yes, but that's not the what. It's "value time" in the big city.

What are your core values? What is it that powers your engine? What do you stand for? Rather than blindly picking those values from thin air or cyberspace, I have compiled a list of 63 values for your review. May I suggest using the *interocular perusal technique*? In other words, eyeball the list to identify your values. You can also add values to that list.

What are the desirable qualities, standards, or principles you value most? For example, they might include lust, gluttony, greed, sloth, wrath, envy, and pride. Kidding. These values will affect your priorities and how you spend your time. To determine your values, follow these five steps:

1. Review the list of values on page 20 carefully.
2. Circle 10 that best capture or represent your own values.
3. Write them in the column ***MY 10***, next to ***BERK'S 10***.
4. Whittle those 10 down to 5.
5. Write those 5 in the column ***MY 5*** in order of priority, highest to lowest, next to ***BERK'S 5***.

Accountability
Achievement
Affection
Altruism
Authenticity
Belonging
Caring
Commitment
Compassion
Competence
Competition
Contentment
Cooperation
Courage
Creativity
Decisiveness
Discipline
Diversity
Effectiveness
Efficiency
Empathy
Excellence
Fairness
Faith
Forgiveness
Freedom
Fun
Generosity
Genuineness
Gratitude
Happiness
Health
Honesty
Honor
Humility
Humor
Initiative
Inspiration
Integrity
Joy
Kindness
Leadership
Love
Loyalty
Money
Nature
Patience
Perseverance
Relationships
Respect
Responsibility
Security
Service
Spirituality
Stability
Status
Success
Teamwork
Tolerance
Tradition
Trust
Wealth
Wisdom

The final list of five should capture the real you. Keep those top five visible and in your mind as you plan your "to-do" list. As you enter assignments and activities in the various time slots daily, weekly, and monthly, your values should be reflected in your priorities. The **A**s and **B**s should reveal your personal core values in some way.

Berk's 10	***My 10***	***Berk's 5***	***My 5***
Trust		Faith	
Respect		Integrity	
Humility		Respect	
Integrity		Humor	
Perseverance		Perseverance	
Compassion			
Humor			
Creativity			
Honesty			
Faith			

2. Specify a Clear Vision

As the pop music hit by Johnny Nash says:

> *I can see clearly now, the rain is gone,*
> *I can see all obstacles in my way*
> *Gone are the dark clouds that had me blind*
> *It's gonna be a bright (bright), bright (bright)*
> *Sun-shiny day.*

Can you see your vision clearly? Maybe you should take off those sunglasses. What is your vision, unique purpose, or mission for your life? "To be a college student." "To have parties with kegs of beer." You're already doing that. Seriously, what is your mission?

Most students have not pondered their life missions. Time to ponder. Now I think we need some ponder music. (Play *Jeopardy!* theme music here.) Your mission is ultra-important because it will be your blueprint for effective time management.

Your mission will reveal

- Where you choose to spend your time, money, and energy;
- Where your heart lies;
- Your passions; and
- Your inspiration and motivation.

Your mission will be your guiding light, beacon, *CSI* Maglite®, compass, GPS, and favorite metaphor that will point you in the direction you're supposed to go. It will dictate your priorities in your daily "to-do" list. Your mission is a living, breathing statement, like your will, but without the inheritance.

Does the mission statement, "To boldly go where no one has gone before!" mean anything to you? Of course not. You probably weren't even conceived when the original TV and movie series *Star Trek* were aired, but you may have seen the 2009 movie version. (Play *Star Trek* theme music here.) It was one of the first adventure programs to feature actors wearing very tight clothing, including one with pointy Vulcan ears, in a spaceship somewhere in a special effects studio in Hollywood.

Probably the most well-known example of a personal mission statement was derived from the *New York Times* best-seller *The Purpose Driven Life* by Rick Warren. He explains how the quest for personal fulfillment, satisfaction, and meaning can be found only in understanding and doing what God placed you on Earth to do. The book's 40 chapters are divided into six major sections, with the following titles:

- What on Earth Am I Here For?
- Purpose #1: You Were Planned for God's Pleasure (Worship)
- Purpose #2: You Were Formed for God's Family (Fellowship)
- Purpose #3: You Were Created to Become Like Christ (Discipleship)
- Purpose #4: You Were Shaped for Serving God (Ministry)
- Purpose #5: You Were Made for a Mission (Mission)

Any one or all of these purposes can serve as a mission statement. The simplest would be: *My purpose is to serve God.* That purpose would then govern the substance of your "to-do" list and all of your assignments, activities, and commitments. Everything would flow from that statement. It becomes ("Oh no, another slew of metaphors?" Yup!) the anchor in your life, the bedrock of your being, the sunshine of your existence, or the epinephrine auto-injector for your bee sting.

Alternatively, you may choose a rather generic statement, such as: *Don't screw up.* It has a definite testosterone-dripping, somewhat negative, ring to it. However, it can serve the purpose.

If the preceding two statements don't fit you, create your own. Begin with your top five values. Express each one or all of them in a statement about your life. Squish them into a summary statement that captures those values and the essence of your mission. That may be your vision.

3. Set Your Personal Goals

Goals are those thick chalk lines at both ends of a football field. If you're not into football, you should be ashamed of yourself. Goals are also those net huts at the ends of soccer, lacrosse, and hockey fields. They're meant to be crossed and penetrated. The object of those games is to kill the student assigned to guard the net with a ball or puck. Remember *The Mighty Ducks* movies or *Bend It Like Beckham*? Well, that was the point: Whack the goalie. (*Digression Alert:* Everyone forgot that, because Brit David Beckham joined the Los Angeles Galaxy soccer team and moved to Beverly Hills with his wife Victoria, the former Posh Spice Girl. *Digression Ends.*) I think we need to get back on track with the subject of this page, which is: Posh Spice.

Goals are also the specific objectives or outcomes that flow from your values and vision statement. They are the results you want to achieve. You can set short-term and long-term goals. Your professors have already set outcomes that you are to master in your respective courses. But those are not yours. *You* must determine the level of mastery or letter grade. That would be short term. Long term would be "graduating in the top 5% of my class."

Take a few minutes to jot down your short-term goals for the current semester related to your courses, health, social activities, family, sports, and any other major aspects of your college life. Here are some examples:

- Get an *A* in psychology.
- Pass physics.
- Get a *B* or higher in economics.
- Get an *A* in biology.
- Get a *B* in U.S. history.
- Jog 30 minutes a day, three times a week.

- Lose 20 pounds.
- Get to semi-final round of spring fencing tournament.
- Spend 1 weekend day a month with my family.
- Become more proficient with PowerPoint® to make presentations.
- Hang with my friends on Friday or Saturday each weekend.
- Audition and win one of the leading roles in the spring musical.
- Become America's next *American Idol* or *Biggest Loser*.

Critique your list to make sure that each outcome is specific, measurable, and realistic within the semester schedule. Break really big goals down into "baby" goals. Your letter grade goals need to be reflected in grades you set for each test and term paper. *A*-grade courses will probably require a lot more time than *B*-grade courses. Choose the most important goals to include in your "to-do" list.

4. Link All of Your Activities to Your Values, Vision, and Goals

Once you have entered the activities for the next day in your planner, make sure your goals are covered and all other entries are consistent with your values and vision. The assignments and commitments in every time slot must be linked to your values, vision, and goals. The congruence among these elements is essential. Otherwise, the preceding exercises were meaningless. And it would be inappropriate to have meaningless time-waster activities this early in a book on time management. Your "to-do" list contains the actions you're going to take to reach your goals. Also, don't forget to recharge your PDA.

5. Use Your Course Syllabi and Other Materials to Plan Your Daily Attack

Your PDA or day-timer probably has a calendar through the 25th century, which should be adequate for this semester's activities. However, to make sure you have all important dates in your long-term as well as short-term plans, gather together all the schedules from your course syllabi, undergraduate catalog, sports events, activities calendar, school newspaper events, and all other resources containing dates and times of noteworthy events in which you might want to participate.

Enter the events from each of these schedules into your planner first. Once the long-term test dates and term paper deadlines, holidays, fall/spring break days, pre-registration dates, university-wide events, and other activities of consequence are recorded, start building your daily "to-do" list. Your daily list of classes, assignments, and personal activities are plugged into time slots not taken by the BIG EVENTS. Collecting the resources above to ensure that you have accounted for all the BIGGIES is essential. That information also provides you with the big picture, though not necessarily in a larger font size, and the little picture. It enables you to see quickly what's coming up each week and to work backwards from the major deadlines to plan your daily tasks. You have it all—daily, weekly, and monthly events for the entire semester at a glance.

6. Don't Take Course Content You Already Know

One of the most common ways to waste time in college is to take courses that cover content you have learned elsewhere. Take as many Advanced Placement Tests or course waiver tests as you can when they are offered. If you know the material, especially in tool areas such as computer literacy, inquire whether a waiver or challenge exam is available.

Another concern is courses with considerable overlapping content. The course syllabi from seemingly different courses can reveal topic coverage redundancy to various degrees. That *content redundancy is also a waste of your time*. If the material was covered in one course in one department, but is repeated in a subsequent course in the same department or in another course in a different department, why sit through the redundant sections?

This is a curriculum issue involving course sequencing, prerequisites, and interdepartmental course redundancy which is not within your purview. However, when these situations arise, you need to talk with the professors or department chairs involved to obtain resolution in your individual case. Schedule appointments with these persons early in the semester to negotiate partial course credit or a content waiver for the redundant material. You have nothing to lose in these meetings and possibly barrels of time to gain. How persuasive can you be? This is a preliminary test of your negotiation skills. If you have a case of significant content redundancy on paper, argue your brief. You never know. You could be a budding debater, politician, lawyer, or Wall Street inside trader.

7. Avoid Course Over-Commitment

Sometimes we can create our own problems. In your zeal to excel in your program, you may overdo it by taking too many credits, too heavy a course load, or by committing to too many clubs, sports, or other activities. Consider a reasonable 15- to 18-credit load balanced against the types of courses available.

Examine your course load carefully in terms of the amount of reading, term papers and projects, and other assignments. This preliminary review is extremely important. Do your homework on these courses in advance. Make believe you're a detective like quirky Adrian Monk or stunning and perceptive Olivia Benson (*Law & Order: SVU*), investigating the optimum combination of courses with the best workload. (Play "Doink! Doink!" sound here.)

Go to the bookstore and check out the number and types (two-inch thick text or 12 paperbacks) of books required for your course choices. Gauge the reading load and the course requirements from the preceding semester's syllabus. Compile all your evidence, weigh all your options, and then determine an appropriate workload and the number of credits to take so you don't burn yourself out.

Once you have a draft of your course load, consider what extracurricular activities would fit into that course schedule. Don't cram everything into your "to-do" list from the outset. Leave space. I know you want to be student government president, first string goalie, Carmen Gia in the spring musical production of *The Producers,* and Posh Spice, but you have four years to do all of that. Spread out your participation in your favorite sports. (Also see #38.)

Use your daily and weekly "to-do" lists to determine what your schedule will look like. Be realistic. Don't forget social activities and personal tasks (see #8 and #9). Try out your schedule for one semester, then fine tune those course and activity entries in your schedule the following semester.

8. Revise Your Plan as Activities and Commitments Arise

Unless you carved your "to-do" schedule into a stone tablet like the *Ten Commandments*, be ready to make changes. Even Moses thought about changing some of the commandments, but decided not to, either because he couldn't find his favorite chisel or he felt the author might get mad. Theologians have never reached consensus on the reason. Whatever, we need to get back to the point of this paragraph, which is: Always pick the right chisel for your "to-do" list.

Activities pop up regularly. There is no way to ensure that the schedule set in your PDA the night before will be unchanged by the following midday. Popping activities can occur at any time. Sometimes you will forget to enter events, your professors may change class assignments and deadlines, social engagements occur without warning, and family emergencies happen.

You must simply DEAL. Revise your PDA schedule and go with the flow. You have no control over these events. What you do control is how you respond to them and the priorities you assign to them in your list. Enter the activities and give them priority letters.

9. Schedule Time for Social Activities

As you already know, college is the best time in your life to play and sow your Quaker Oats®. WROOOONNG! It's a time to prepare for a career in English, U.S. history, chemistry, political science, or economics, and eventually get a job in your dad's law firm or hardware store. (*Time out:* Guess what time it is? It's "Tool Time!") Hammers and screwdrivers will be your tools. "Stop fooling around. This is serious business." Sorry. Your PDA schedule reflects your commitment to your classes and to completing all of the assignments on time.

However, something's missing. What's wrong with this picture so far? "My dad was the CEO of a big, evil corporation." Okay, I was wrong about your dad. What's missing is *Animal House*-type fun. Toga parties, pizza and beer, controlled substances, and rowdy, rude, and crude behavior—all of those things you couldn't do at home, at least not until your parents went on vacation. (*Note*: I do not condone any of the aforementioned legal or illegal activities. They're mentioned only to grab your attention and get through this paragraph because I noticed your eyelids closing.) Well, maybe this is a little exaggerated, maybe not, but you get the point.

You need to carve out time in your schedule for those social activities that you enjoy and for having "fun." Those activities are therapeutic—they release stress, tension, and anxiety. They can keep you sane. Spread them out and try to schedule them when you need them most. You may look forward to attending Saturday football games, weekday basketball games, theater performances, and other events every week. They can help recharge your batteries to tackle the assignments or test review that are waiting back at your study room. Also, don't forget to plan trips with your buddies to expensive resorts using your parents' timeshares for winter and spring breaks.

If you are introverted, not socially inclined, or have weak interpersonal skills, you still need these breaks. Consider chatting with someone online—a family member, a pet, or an inflatable person of your choice. Go to a movie, concert, or the theater. Mark these activities in your "to-do" list. They're important elements in your schedule. They can serve as distractions and provide perspective in your college life so that you don't become a recluse and spend all of your time inflating make-believe roommates.

10. Block Appointment Times With Yourself

This strategy is one of the well-hidden, self-serving secrets of people who achieve peak productivity. They block time for themselves throughout their schedules so they won't waste it. These blocks are not necessarily for social or "fun" activities. They are designed to make sure you use your time wisely and do not squander blocks of time in which nothing was scheduled. Squandering is bad.

Review your daily, weekly, and monthly schedule for the current semester as it is now written. You will notice time blocks that are blank—no classes, no assignments, no studying, no sports events, no parties, no nothing. And I don't mean the hours of 12 midnight to 6 A.M.

What are you going to do during those times? Most students don't think about that or even care. Those blocks are your valuable times. If you don't schedule them in your "to-do" list and assign a priority letter, when those times arrive, you'll probably (You know. Say it with me: "Squander") or fritter them away with some mindless activity, such as inflating your plastic roommate or aimlessly meandering down the highways and byways of your residence hall. What a waste! You should be ashamed of yourself, especially after our discussion of squandering.

The alternative is to plug into those blocks specific tasks or activities that you *HAVE* to complete and those that you *WANT* to do. Here is your opportunity to go beyond your immediate plans. These blocks can provide the jumpstart you always wanted to get ahead in your assignments instead of just keeping up. Wouldn't that be a pip? Or, what about participating in one of the team sports, like crew, jousting, *Lost*, or *Survivor: College Edition*, that you never had time for previously? Maybe auditioning for the spring play or musical would give you a new outlet for your talents.

All of these blocked times should be treated as inviolate, just as any other important, high priority activity in your "to-do" list is treated. Those times are committed. Once they are in your schedule, you should have few loose, unassigned, or unplanned times. The added blocks should soon be evidenced by your increased productivity.

While we're talking about loose blocks, you might want to start thinking about the summer. Unless you plan on taking some courses to pull ahead in your program or to lighten your fall load, you will have lots of time blocks to fill. A job will consume many of them, but you will still have others. Plan what you are going to do over the summer months during the beginning of the spring semester so you have adequate time to sort out the options. Don't waste that time squandering, frittering, or meandering. You already did that in paragraph three. You'll regret it.

11. Follow Your Daily Plans as Closely as Possible

This section is where the rubber meets the proverbial roadkill. Typing your "to-do" list is extremely important, but following through with those commitments is even more important. That's why you entered them in your PDA. Always have your schedule with you so you can check the big picture for the current day as well as view what's next. It is your lifeline guide to getting through your courses and personal activities.

Glancing at it throughout the day will help you stay on track and adhere to your schedule. Once you get used to this schedule, you'll be amazed at how much you can accomplish. At 10 o'clock at night, you'll look back at your PDA list and say: "How did I meander through all of those **C**s and forget about the **A**s? What was I thinking? I'm a moron! That's all I accomplished?" Kidding. A little PDA humor. You'll really say: "Wow! I can't believe I completed all of the **A**s and all but two of the **B**s. I can whip them out tomorrow." Now you're ready to plan your next day's list. Fill in the uncompleted **B**s and **C**s in the open slots between the **A**s. You're all set. How long did that take? Seeeeeeee! Trust me.

12. Review Your Plans Frequently and Make Adjustments as Necessary

As you wander through your schedule, make adjustments as new events arise or activities change. It's probably advisable to review your daily list at midday and in the evening to make sure everything is on target and you didn't forget anything.

At the end of the week or on the weekend, review your weekly and monthly schedules to account for any changes that may have occurred as well as to furnish an overview for the major deadlines and tests coming up. Once you see them, you may feel additional preparation is needed hither and yon. Schedule whatever prep times are required in the open time blocks.

Also, identify any wasteful and unproductive activities that may have leaked into your schedule. Patch the leaks and eliminate those activities to free up time for what's important. You're in control, but plan accordingly.

You're going into battle every day. Be prepared to engage every activity in your schedule. You have to decide how you want to walk into that chemistry midterm—loaded for bear or for muskrat. (*Note:* See. Now you know why your PDA sports that protective cover made of aircraft-strength double-plated titanium.)

3

Time-Saving Studying Techniques

13. Tackle One Task at a Time

Multitasking has become a natural way of life. There is so much to do that it seems like the only option. In fact, surveys of this (Inter)Net Generation of college students indicate that they are especially adept at multitasking with multiple forms of media. They can play video games on their PCs while talking on their BlackBerrys® with one ear, listening to music on their iPods with the other ear, while waxing their Mini Coopers and Smart ForTwos with their other ear. That's amazing!

Multitasking provides the illusion that you are able to do more than one thing at a time, thereby increasing your efficiency and productivity. *Au contraire*! (A French expression meaning, literally, "Your shorts are on backwards.") There is no evidence to support this brief, I mean belief. The research on multitasking reveals that it actually decreases productivity. Switching back and forth between two or more tasks takes time. Further, none of the tasks receives your full attention.

You'll get more done when you focus on one activity at a time. In other words, as you review your "to-do" list, tackle one **A**. Don't bounce back and forth between two **A** assignments. Give one **A** your undivided attention and effort until it is finished. Then move on to the next **A** and so on. Don't let any interruptions pull your focus. Note the nature of the interruption, and get to it later after the **As** are completed. Also, concentrate on the outcome of each assignment, such as "read chapters 6 and 7 in economics," rather than "read econ for 1 hour." Follow these techniques and you will be whizzing through your "to-do" list.

14. Attack the Most Difficult Task First

When you have to choose among several subjects to start studying or whether to write an essay or term paper, it is natural for you to go to the fridge first and make a salami sandwich on rye with mustard, lettuce, and a juicy pickle. No. Actually I meant to say: Pick the easiest first, the one that even Dopey in *Snow White* could complete. It's motivating, energizing, and satisfying to accomplish a task that you know you can complete. Conquering that book review builds confidence and self-esteem. "Wait. Excuse me. Time out. What happened to the salami sandwich?" That was a joke. "You're kidding me." Right. "But that sandwich made me hungry." Go make one. We now resume this paragraph somewhere near the end. Unfortunately, that victory doesn't help you complete the toughest subject. The statistics problems still have to be solved. Putting them on the back burner delays their completion and puts you at risk of not doing them at all, especially if you run out of time and are functioning in crisis mode.

Start with your most difficult assignment and a salami sandwich, the one that's screaming: "YIIIKES! Do me. Do me NOOOW!" (*Note:* The screaming is coming from the assignment, not the sandwich. Had it been the sandwich, there would have been mustard on it.) You need to totally focus on those statistics problems. Don't even think about your other assignments until stat is done. Consider the feeling you will have when you finish the stat problems. That's empowerment. When those problems have been completed, your confidence and self-esteem levels will be through the roof, shooting waaaay beyond the levels previously attained after you wrote the book review for English literature. Plus, the worst is over. Now the remaining assignments are a piece of cake, or rather, a salami sandwich. You can do those with your left hemisphere tied behind your back.

15. Seek Help With Tough Assignments If You Need It

You will be able to complete most of the difficult subjects and assignments. However, once in a while an assignment comes along, and you don't have a clue what to do. It's like walking into a wall, SMACK!!, but without the bruising. This could be because of an unclear explanation in class, an uninterpretable text, not being in class when the material was covered, or being too drunk or high to remember. Whatever the reason for your lack of understanding, take action.

When you have this close encounter of the insurmountable kind, don't sit at your desk and waste time staring at it. It will jump up and bite you, like Jaws. (Play theme music from *Jaws* here.) Kidding. Of course, it won't, but it will eat your salami sandwich. Staring at it won't change the difficulty of the assignment. It will not be intimidated by your facial expressions.

Seek help immediately from a classmate, teaching assistant, lab assistant, your professor, or Dr. Phil. Contact someone quickly so you can get the work completed on time. Don't fall behind or hesitate to get assistance. If you ask a classmate for help, be prepared to offer your time and expertise in return on a subject in which he or she needs assistance. This reciprocity is reasonable. It depends entirely on your unique relationship and the study arrangement that the two of you plan.

If your problem reoccurs and turns into a weekly event because the subject matter doesn't draw on your strengths, line up a tutor or join a study group (see #31). Struggling through the course by yourself can end up in disaster. Use the resources available to you. Everyone has strengths and weaknesses and, sooner or later, he or she meets his or her match. Remember, this paragraph is not about dating; it's about lining up. Make sure you have regular help with your assignments and that those study slots are entered into your "to-do" list. Allow adequate time for these **A** slots.

16. Chop Up BIG Projects Into Bite-Size Morsels

Semester-long papers, research projects, and the like can be difficult to tackle and may appear overwhelming. As well they should, because they are monster assignments with the express purpose of devouring innocent, unsuspecting students in one gulp. At least that's how they usually appear when you read their descriptions and grading criteria in the syllabus. You're probably thinking: "Why me?" It's like eating a walrus. After you remove it from your grill, which is the size of Toledo, where do you begin?

Once the monster effect has subsided, read the specifications for the paper or project very carefully. Don't let the 20- to 30-page requirements disturb you. Put the project into perspective by chopping it up into small, bite-size pieces.

For example, you might focus on the meat—the synthesis of the research or opinions on the topic—first. Create the skeleton outline of the material you need to synthesize. Using that outline, write a draft of the meat for each section, one at a time. This is usually the hardest part. Try to spread out these sections over several weeks. Schedule small writing segments you can handle. Think small. When one section is done, start on the next. Repeat this process until every section is in draft form. Now you have some flesh on your boney outline. Finally, it's time to kill this metaphor. WHAM!!

You can produce a large work using that piecemeal technique. What's left after you have written the "meat" are editing the total package and writing a beginning and end to the paper. The latter will probably jump out of your PC or Mac screen. A similar strategy, known as the "Swiss Cheese Method," has also been recommended for dealing with large writing assignments. It is described in #28. For other cheese methods, consult your FAVE deli.

The acknowledgments, which you probably skipped, and those in my previous books describe how and where I write. Please take advantage of ALL the places you can write your paper morsels other than in the comfort of your room. Strategies #24 and #25 provide extensive lists of possible writing venues where you can get a lot of your writing completed. You'll be surprised at how much work you can accomplish while waiting for your car repair or in the doctor's office. Take your laptop everywhere you go and just write.

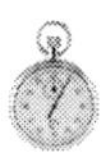

17. Pinpoint Your Best Time to Study

Are you a morning or night person? Do you wander the countryside throughout the night with Dracula, Michael Myers, or Jason Voorhees? Or are you in a near-coma-like sleep in your bed dreaming of sugarplum fairies, Angelina Jolie, or Mario Lopez?

Plan your schedule around your high and low times. Your prioritized work times should be custom tailored to your peak work times. When do you have the most energy? During which hours of the day are you fully charged to do chemistry? "No time!" Ha ha. I know you're kidding. I understand. But you must have a prime time to hunker down and complete your readings without dozing.

The research indicates that your peak performance naturally occurs between 6 A.M. and noon when your mental and physical energy levels are highest. If you're not a "morning" person, I know that's bad news. But you need to get an early start to your day. Although you may not be an early bird or a worm, you'll accomplish a lot more throughout the day if you can roll out of the sack by 6 or 7 A.M. However, this can be altered by what you eat and drink (see # 43).

Make sure the most important, urgent, less desirable, and most boring, miserable, and difficult **A**s in your "to-do" list are scheduled during your peak times. Doesn't that sound palatable? Start with those **A**s. You'll need to be at the top of your game to conquer them. Once those **A**s are done, your motivation will be high to hurdle the other **A**s and then the **B**s, which will be easier. This will be during your low energy time. But there's always that second wind or dose of caffeine to pump you through that period. The more frequently you push yourself through this schedule, the easier it will become.

18. Study in Short Time Blocks With Short Breaks in Between

How do you get the biggest bang for your block? Limit it to two hours. Focusing on one subject for two hours can be very productive. However, even with a protein meal and caffeine beverages, fatigue is inevitable. Your eyeballs may drop out of their sockets—SPROOOIIING!—and dangle down to your kneecaps by their optic nerves. That will usually occur after the two-hour time block. Once your attention drifts and you start thinking of Budweiser® Clydesdale commercials or an upcoming rehearsal for *Les Misérables*, take a break, but not an extended vacation in Orlando.

Do something different for a few minutes, such as exercise (a 10-minute walk, jog, or bike ride), play with your Portuguese water dog or iguana, punch a bag, eat a Cadbury® bar or quart of Rocky Road, or play a video game or exergame such as *Wii Fit*. These are your possible rewards for studying. You can look forward to these breaks, but remember that you will have to resume studying. Regular breaks will improve your concentration, motivation, and performance. Your studying will be effective time spent, not just going through the motions. If you exercise, you will also feel an increase in your energy level that may last until your next break.

When you schedule your study blocks for each course, space them out across the week. Don't smush them into just two or three days. Chunk your studying into small blocks every day. Alternate different course study blocks throughout each day; for example, physics, English, Russian, and statistics. Don't schedule similar subjects back to back. Studying two math or language courses in a row, even with a break, can create content confusion. Mix it up and spread it out across the week.

19. Make Sure Your Surroundings Are Conducive to Studying

Find your *sanctum sanctorum* (Latin words meaning, literally, "There's a weasel on your head"). You need a hideaway, a shelter, a place to study where you can go and not be disturbed. You say, "There is no such place on my campus. It's noisy everywhere—in the residence halls, library, classrooms, and restrooms, even under the trees and shrubbery." I get it. I know conversations between grasshoppers and mosquitoes can be annoying. Okay, let's consider this tip a goal. Here's the *IDEAL*: A comfortable, quiet, soundproof, bombproof, and family-proof room with good lighting and no bed or any other furniture that can be misconstrued as a bed. (See also #26 and #27.)

Based on these criteria, it is unlikely that your room will pass mustard or any other condiment. "You had to mention mustard, salamiboy! Now I'm hungry again." Maybe the library has carrels hidden in the deep recesses of the university catacombs or a small, sealed-off study room with an electrical outlet. (*Note:* It's usually not advisable to run a 3000-foot bright orange extension cord from your room to the library to power your laptop. Somebody might notice, plus you'll lose some power over a half mile.) Locate the best place possible, where you can go every day to realize your peak performance. This is where your battle plans for conquering those **A**s and **B**s will be executed. Put on your headphones and get to work.

If you commute to school from a home with a family and a Portuguese water dog, the preceding scenario may be unrealistic. If you have an office at home where you can work uninterrupted, go for it. If not, be prepared to test your limits of concentration. In other words, visualize helicopter friends and/or family, but especially your kids, hovering over you in your house. Under these conditions, you have few options. Just hunker down and focus the best you can. (*Note:* I realize that you've been doing a lot of hunkering lately, but your family will be sooo proud. Keep it up.)

Try to mentally and physically shut out the distractions using your special Stealth Study Strategies™. The SSS™ approach allows you to get your work done with big or little people present. Imagine your Stealth-self sitting at your kitchen table, munching on invisible chocolate chip cookies, sipping hot chocolate, and chugging along with your chemistry problems. Your kids can't see you, yet they know you're in the room. Kinda surreal, huh? If you can knock off your **A**s in this situation, you could probably study anywhere. Go for it!

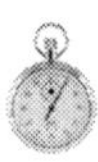

20. Try to Stay 1 to 3 Days Ahead in Your Assignments

There's no worse feeling than being behind in your coursework, unprepared, pressured all of the time, and always playing catch-up. Well, maybe there is: Trailing throughout any ball game, hurling chunks over the side of a boat, or being tortured by Jack Bauer on *24* is no picnic either. Being behind can produce increased levels of stress, tension, and anxiety, and feelings of loss of control and being overwhelmed. That's not a positive state of mental health.

However, once you put some of the suggestions in the preceding pages into action, you will be in a position not only to come from behind but also to pull ahead. The various strategies described in this book converge on one goal—to free up time so you can go to toga parties. TŌ GA! TŌ GA! Not exactly. It's to manage your time efficiently so you are in control of your schedule. That may result in free time to do those things you *want* to do.

How do you get ahead? Here are five steps to follow to Togaland:

1. Before you can be ahead, you need to be on schedule. If your "to-do" list is set up daily and followed religiously, you should be up to date with all of your **A** and **B** commitments.
2. Review your weekly plan for empty time blocks, including the weekend.
3. Without cutting social activities, ball games, dinners at the White House with the Obama's water dog Bo, and similar events, start filling the blocks with assignments from the next one to three days. The more you can fill, the further ahead you will be, at least on paper.
4. Prioritize those assignments with **A**s or **B**s in the context of the rest of your activities.

5. Now that you have a plan with the "ahead" assignments integrated into your daily and weekly lists, follow it. Do what you've been doing, except now you will automatically be ahead in those courses and assignments where that's possible. Of course, the design of some courses won't permit jumping ahead as easily. Do it where you can.

There are four major benefits to systematically planning to be ahead in most of your courses: (1) it provides a psychological edge and stress reducer, (2) it's a confidence builder that produces a feeling of empowerment over your college work, (3) it furnishes a cushion in case of an unexpectedly heavy workload, personal illness, or family emergency, and (4) it will free up time so you can eat your salami sandwich and pickle. You've built up advance course-load credit by completing assignments before they're due. What a relief. You'll be thankful for that cushion one day.

21. Attend ALL of Your Classes

Your parents or you are paying wads of money for your courses. Maybe you should attend your classes. Ya think? Yes, I know they're boring, but at least you can catch up on your sleep. Going to classes where the professor reads PowerPoint® slides to you as though you were three years old can be frustrating. I can empathize. But try to get the most out of your classes.

Aside from getting some sleep and your money's worth out of your college education, there are other reasons to consider. Going to class (a) helps you to understand your professor, maybe; (b) provides you with information and classroom experiences first-hand; (c) saves you the time of getting possibly incomplete information from secondhand notes or a poor recording; and (d) gives you the best estimate of the work load and content difficulty so that you can prioritize the importance and urgency of the assignments in your "to-do" list. Attending class can not only improve your time management of the course requirements, but it can also increase your achievement and how much you learn. Of course, that depends on the particular course and what you are able to get out of it.

22. Take Thoughtful Notes in Class

Don't write down or type everything in sight and sound like a maniac. Relax. LISTEN CAREFULLY to discern what's important. Based on the information in your syllabus and other course materials, be prepared for the topic to be covered. Review your notes and assigned readings so you'll have a rough idea of what is coming. *The more you know what to expect in advance, the better your notes will be.* You will already have some familiarity with the material and a context for the content being spewed. It will make more sense from the get-go as you are recording it.

What points are emphasized? Watch your professor's body language. Pick up on cues such as voice inflection, pauses, repetition of points, and summaries. Try to "psych out" your professor. Jot down as much meat as possible, but pay particular attention to the content in the middle of the lecture. You usually remember best the beginning and end. Use abbreviations to cut down on typing. Just get as much as you can. The notes should be comprehensive. If there are gaps, you can fill them in later.

Effective note taking can save you from spending time figuring out what someone else wrote and why they wrote it. If you miss class, get several sets of notes. Everyone takes notes differently. If you drifted, napped, or tuned out and missed some notes, check with your buddies to fill in the gaps. Make sure your notes are as complete as possible.

Review your notes right after class when everything is fresh. Spend at least 10 minutes to edit, highlight key points, outline, and summarize the content. Compare your notes to other classmates' notes to add missing material. This short "editorial review" period after class can be an invaluable time saver later when you have to prepare for a test on that content.

 23. Use Tickler Files

The name is intriguing, isn't it? These files probably won't make you laugh, but if you use them as intended, they may give you a modest level of joy. This technique is recommended by just about every time management expert. It is an organizing system for handling course materials, articles, notes, CDs, DVDs, flash drives, and other small matter you're not sure where to file. Here are the steps:

1. Get 12 orange (or another bright color) folders and label them January through December.
2. Get 31 lime green folders and label them 1–31 for every day in a month, except February which has 32. Haha. That's an example of calendar humor.

That's it. Now suppose you cut out an article in the newspaper related to your political science term paper on the federal budget for HIV/AIDS research. The term paper is due in two months, but you need to gather materials by the 15th. Put the article in the number 15 file folder for February.

Check your tickler file every day for items that need attention. Schedule a regular time slot in your "to-do" list for the file. When February 15 rolls around, that article will automatically pop up. You can defer doing anything with the article until the next month, or put it in a different folder. As you empty a day's folder by acting on the popping material or moving it to a later date, move the empty folder to next month's folder. The 31 folders will rotate through the cycle every month. How about putting your bills in the appropriate folders so they will be paid on time? Those will really pop.

What an efficient system to keep track of anything that isn't in your PDA! It can reduce the clutter of unfiled papers or disks, provide you with automatic memory, and supplement your "to-do" list to improve your daily planning.

Despite these benefits, there's a problem if you don't like popping or you're a normal residence hall-rooming college student—You don't have a palatial office with file cabinets. Your measly little room may not be big enough. Tickler files require space. If you don't have it, it won't work. However, before discarding the tickler concept, try a few plastic containers from The Container Store to store your files. They're more flexible and space friendly than steel or cardboard cabinets. They can be stacked and placed in different areas, such as under your bed, if there's any space left.

Alternatively, if you do not have adequate space or a file cabinet to use folders regularly, you can set up a *computerized tickler system.* Simply enter a reminder on your calendar to work on a particular task. You can enter several reminders, if necessary, including contact information, location of files, and other important information. Flat, not lumpy, files could also be scanned for convenience in one location on your hard drive.

24. Carry Study Materials When Traveling

If you really want to get ahead in your course load, this time saver is *one of the most effective techniques you can possibly use.* Whenever you leave your room to go anywhere, take a bag or backpack with course materials and laptop with you. Don't leave home without something, but don't take everything, especially those vertebrae-breaking, cartilage-tearing monster textbooks. Almost everywhere you go will require wait time, which you could use to finish reading two chapters in your psychology book, computing all of the math problems, writing a section of a term paper, finishing other assignments on your list, or, maybe, adding a few items to your "to-do" list. Estimate your wait time to decide how much and what type of coursework to take.

As you travel to your destination, your mode of transportation will allow you a variety of opportunities to catch up on your assignments. There are four major traveling options:

- ***On foot***—walking or jogging—you might want to stop in the park and take a break to read under a tree or near a lake or active volcano.
- ***On wheels***, such as biking, skateboarding, or driving, you can always stop or end up in a traffic jam, which is the perfect time to dig out those biology notes and figure out what you have to do in the lab. If you're traveling by bus, train, 18-wheeler, RV, mobile home, or army tank, be prepared with lots of course materials. There's a good chance that you will be waiting before your trip and after as well, especially if someone is supposed to pick you up. If you end up stranded on a remote, deserted country road in the fog and rain for hours or days, you'll have plenty of work time; that is, until you're eaten by a bear or mountain lion. (*Note:* Always carry a *CSI*-type flashlight or miner's headlight for reading, a salami sandwich for eating, plus a knife and gun for defending

yourself.) Of course, the time on the trip itself will permit you to do a lot of reading and/or writing, unless, of course, you get motion sickness.

- ***On wings***, if you're on the way to the airport, take plenty of work with you. You could have tons of time waiting for your initial flight and then more for your connections or the ones you missed, plus all of the time on the flight itself. With the trend in airline delays constantly increasing for whatever reason, you quite possibly may be able to complete your assignments for the whole semester or year if you pick the right Thanksgiving, winter break, or spring break flight. This same advice also applies to hang gliding, parachuting, parasailing, skydiving, and bungee jumping, though with less available time.
- ***On rudders***, once you've started up the motor on your speed boat and ride the waves or set sail on the open choppy seas, you'll probably throw up. Wait, that's not the end to that sentence. I seem to have misplaced it. Oh, here it is: you will have plenty of time on the water to work on whittling down those **A**s and **B**s, unless you're a barf bag. Get a patch. If you're planning on fishing, you'll get to the **C**s with time to spare. Use every opportunity you have to complete the tasks on your list. You will return refreshed and relieved that the stressful burden of assignments has been lifted from your shoulders. Ahhhhhh. I already feel relaxed. None of these feelings will apply if you hurled your guts on these trips.

 25. Carry Study Materials to Every Destination

Now let's consider your destination. If you haven't completed all of your assignments for the current year while traveling, and you haven't been eaten by a mountain lion, you will have several other opportunities for studying at many of the routine places you go every day. For some of these, such as the grocery store or bank, a paperback from English lit or history will be adequate; for others, such as a doctor's appointment or the police station, you might consider packing everything. Kidding. You can leave your gym bag in your room.

Here is a starter list of 20 opportunities. I'm sure you can think of other places to add to this list.

- Standing in line at the grocery, clothing, or any other store
- Standing in line for concert or ballgame tickets
- Standing in line at the bank or post office
- Waiting for your laundry at the Laundromat or a friend's apartment
- Waiting for your food in a restaurant if your friend forgets to meet you
- Waiting for your friend and while eating in the cafeteria or coffee shop
- Waiting at the student health center on campus until someone shows up
- Waiting for your car to be repaired
- Waiting in your car at drive-through banks and fast-food restaurants
- Waiting for your residence hall room to be repaired after a tree fell on it or a truck drove through it
- Waiting to be picked up on the remote, deserted country road in the fog and rain before being devoured alive by a werewolf or Hugh Jackman

- Waiting for sports events to begin or during boring periods at baseball, football, or basketball games
- Waiting in line for Passport Control as you enter the airport of a foreign city, such as Moscow, Kiev, or Dubai; the one exception is Amsterdam (*Note*: There is no line at Passport Control or Immigration at Schiphol Airport in Amsterdam. You just whiz through. What could you possibly bring into The Netherlands that isn't legal and on display there already?)
- Sitting in the waiting room for a doctor's or dentist's appointment
- Waiting at the police station or in jail on DUI or drug charges until someone bails you out (*Note:* Armed robbery and other felonies will have longer wait times.)
- Waiting at the courthouse for someone to pick you up after you are released on your own recognizance
- Waiting in the hospital emergency room (*Note:* Try not to get blood, vomit, or other bodily fluids on your books or notes, especially if you borrowed them.)
- Waiting for surgery to begin (*Note:* Once your IV sedative or anesthesia has begun, don't bother reading; working on stat or organic chemistry problems is okay.)
- During your recuperation in the hospital (*Note:* If organs or body parts are removed, plan for pain medications and long wait times with lots of course materials.)
- During dull and boring parties (or just leave)

Studying during any of the aforementioned travel or destination opportunities could put you way ahead in your assignments with gobs of time to spend on activities you want to do. Working during those dead and usually wasted times can markedly change your "to-do" list so you are whipping through those **A**s and **B**s across an entire week. What a relief it would be to start the weekend without the stress of those assignments on your head. You can relax and go to the football game and party and really enjoy them.

26. Eliminate Distractions

What distracts you from concentrating on your work? Those evil little thoughts racing through your brain? Maybe some non-evil thoughts? What stimulated those thoughts? Whatever those thoughts might be, it is clear that some students are easily distracted. However, you know students who study with TV, radio, or music blasting, the Jonas Brothers singing in their room, or jumping up and down at a Beyoncé concert. The rule of thumb is: *Total focus usually requires the absence of distracting visual or auditory stimuli.*

Distractions are very personal. It's all about you. What conditions do you need to maximize your productivity? Any stimulus that pulls your focus away from your reading or breaks your concentration while writing can rob you of valuable study time. You will probably have to shut down your iPhone or BlackBerry® completely; vibrate isn't an option. Try airplane mode. Turn off everything that could potentially create a distraction. Put on headphones or a soundproof helmet with CDC-type contamination suit and get to work.

The above suggestions may be unrealistic for many of you in family situations, such as those described in #19 and #27, plus contamination suits may not be available in your size. You may need to adapt to your available study environment with the SSS™ approach or some other chameleon technique to shut out the distractions around you. It's harder to do, but, with plenty of practice, you may be even more productive than in a quiet room.

27. Minimize Electronic and Human Interruptions

Interruptions can steal your valuable study time by derailing your focus, killing your momentum, and decreasing your productivity. Those consequences are ugly. Interruptions in any form are monster, evil time wasters because they pull you away from your meticulously planned "to-do" list. The most common interruptions include

1. Electronic communications (e-mail, TM, phone calls, etc.) from a significant other, friends, and/or family members
2. Face-to-face communications with drop-in visitors
3. Face-to-face communications with your roommate
4. Face-to-face communications with family members at home
5. Face-to-face communications with aliens
6. Face-to-face communications with your inflatable friend

As you can tell from the list, the interruptions originate with the people and aliens in your life, real and unreal. If you are an unsociable, obnoxious, irritating, abrasive, annoying, lonely hermit, interruptions shouldn't be a major problem in your college life. On the other hand, if you are a sociable, gregarious, people-person with loads of friends, and a former winner of the Mr. or Ms. Congeniality title, you will have serious interruption problems.

Relationships can be messy, especially if you have a whackadoodle roommate or two. The people closest to you should be "Mirandized" about your study schedule and your peak times when you don't want to be disturbed. The only exceptions would be emergencies or life-threatening situations. When you are working in your prime times, your phone should be off and return calls,

TMs, and e-mail should be checked at the times you decide. Be inaccessible. You should be in control of all electronic and face-to-face communications during your concentrated high importance and urgent **A** activities. Of course, your mother will disagree, but she will have to "deal" with the reality of your new life sooner or later.

That advice is appropriate for campus life situations. But what about commuters who live at home with lively family-type people who compete for your attention? As indicated in strategies #19 and #26, you need to adapt to those situations differently. You are studying under real combat conditions, which will require greater powers of concentration and focus. Eliminating face-to-face communications is not an option, especially if you are living with children, pets, livestock, and/or aliens. They will demand more attention than your significant other and create more interruptions. Just keep refocusing on your work. It'll get done.

28. Overcome Procrastination

Most students procrastinate on completing assignments at one time or another. It is so easy to slip into that behavior, because it's the default to doing something—to do nothing until later. Failure to do your assignments can have serious academic consequences. If you delay acting on your tasks occasionally or get a little lazy sometimes, but can catch up and turn on all cylinders when it's necessary, you probably don't have a problem. However, *if those delays occur regularly and you're always behind in your assignments, there is cause for concern.* Not doing your work is a time waster. What are you doing in place of what you should be doing? Perhaps trying to figure out the grammatical structure of that sentence.

If you are an admitted, self-confessed procrastinator, you need help. You will not survive the demands of college. The rest of this section is designed to give you some guidance. If you are not a procrastinator, but have a friend who is, you can either continue reading with the goal of possibly counseling him or her, or just skip to strategy #29.

Fear of failure is frequently the primary cause of procrastination. Subjects or assignments that seem difficult or overwhelming can be the objects of this fear. Rather than trying to tackle them, you just push them aside and avoid them altogether. Once this procrastination begins with one subject, it can become a cycle that's repeated with other subjects. It will be increasingly difficult to break this cycle.

The issue is how to regain control and conquer the subjects that produced these symptoms. If you cannot resolve the problem by yourself, it might be worth seeing a counselor. Here are seven steps you can try:

1. ***Identify the source of the problem***—fear of rejection, failure, responsibility, criticism, disappointing others, imperfection, making a mistake, change, inadequacy, or success; feeling overwhelmed; desire for attention; boring or difficult tasks; resentment; unclear goals.
2. ***Break down your tasks into subtasks***—write down the reading assignments, essays, problems, or term papers that you are avoiding. Reduce the assignments to small, manageable subtasks that seem reasonable. Seeing these tiny chunks as molehills rather than as mountains can break the inactivity-avoidance cycle (see #6).
3. ***Apply the "Swiss Cheese Method"*** (Alan Lakein)—when a term paper or project appears overwhelming or boring, poke holes in it. Do the easy, small tasks that take only a few minutes first. Continue to poke until most of the work is done. The completion of all of the holes and poking will motivate you to take on the tougher, more complex tasks that remain (also see #16).
4. ***Focus on the outcomes and deadlines***—set attainable deadlines in your "to-do" list consistent with the real deadlines in your syllabus. Express the assignments as outcomes to be finished within the time blocks. For example, state "Hi-lite and outline chap. 6" instead of "read chap. 6." Be specific and realistic with each task so you don't backslide into avoidance behavior again.
5. ***Review your daily, weekly, and semester schedules regularly***—make sure your short-term assignments and deadlines are on target with the long-term deadlines for term papers and tests. Make adjustments daily to stay on course. Pace yourself for the whole semester; don't crunch tasks together in tight timeframes which you may not be able to

complete. Been there, done that. Don't drift back into your old behaviors.

6. ***Find an accountability partner***—choose a close buddy, your roommate, or family member to whom you can report your successes and failures at the end of each week (see also #30). The fear of embarrassment from not fulfilling the commitments on your "to-do" list can provide an additional incentive to stay on task and meet your deadlines.
7. ***Reward yourself for small and large victories***—celebrate your wins. Reward the new *you* for overcoming your procrastination. The preceding steps represent a *time management makeover* of you. That's a significant achievement by itself.

29. Reduce Unscheduled or Unplanned Activities

If your "to-do" list is packed with activities and you have blocked time for others, you shouldn't have many slots available for unscheduled or unplanned activities. Your goal should be to fill your schedule with as many **A**s and **B**s as possible so you are constantly working through your tasks. Only those unexpected activities that are important should be given slots in your schedule. Where to fill in those slots is up to you.

30. Find an Accountability Partner

It's tough to go through college alone. There are so many demands on your time from your courses, sports, and social activities that I'm writing this book to free up as much of your time as possible. However, the commitment to write the five-minute "to-do" list every day and then follow it can be challenging for some of you. You have to be well-organized and self-disciplined to stay on track. Having some form of accountability is one way to prevent you from straying from your appointments.

Choosing an accountability partner should not be taken lightly. That person needs to be as committed to his or her goals and plan as you are, although the goals and plan are different. You should both share several of the values identified previously (see #1). Trust and integrity are super-important. If either party lies to the other about what he or she did during the week, the commitment is broken.

You are baring your academic and personal work schedule to each other. Sharing that information reveals your flaws, mistakes, and embarrassment when you have not completed your tasks, as well as your strengths through those that were completed. Acceptance of each other's imperfection is critical. It should be okay to fail or not meet a deadline occasionally. Your openness and honesty are essential for the accountability to have meaning and teeth. Ultimately, you both have the same long-term goal: your diplomas.

Make an effort to schedule an accountability meeting in your "to-do" lists at the end of each week. Discussing what worked and didn't work should result in adjustments to the lists for the following week and a mini-celebration of your victories. Knowing you have to answer to someone every week about your accomplishments can propel you forward to work harder and perform better.

Trying to do this alone makes you more vulnerable to temptations that can yank you off track. Find a partner who will not allow you to be yanked. If a real partner is hard to find, get an inflatable or imaginary one.

31. Join a Real or Virtual Study Group

Instead of one accountability partner, this strategy kicks it up three- to fivefold. The study group is one of the most effective and efficient vehicles for covering a lot of course material. It provides automatic accountability for each member, plus it often requires you to extend your limits.

The persistent and often intractable problem in assembling the group has been the excruciatingly long audition process, not unlike *American Idol* or *So You Think You Can Dance!* WROOONG! The problem is finding three to five students willing to commit their minds, bodies, hearts, and spleens to do the work and meet regularly. If you can recruit at least two students who are willing to sacrifice themselves for the cause, you'll have a triad. Try it.

The group can meet in person or online once or twice a week. Schedule these sessions in your "to-do" list. You must do your fair share of the work, whether it is outlining chapters, summarizing notes, preparing review questions, preparing gourmet meals and snacks, vacuuming after each meeting, or some other contribution. One of the major benefits is the discussion of topics. The interaction on the course material allows you to explain concepts, teach each other material, and raise questions to clarify points. You can gain a deeper understanding of the content rather than just memorizing facts.

This group saves you time in studying the same content on your own, and it facilitates more thorough learning by making each member accountable. It also provides mutual support to get through tough courses, such as statistics, organic chemistry, pathophysiology, taxidermy, tax evasion, and insider trading, rather than going it alone.

 32. Organize Your Course Materials

You have so many books, so little time. Does your room need an Extreme Makeover? Could you be one of the "messy people" guests on *Oprah*? How do you organize all of that stuff?

Keep the materials for each course separate. Organize the *text-based courses*, such as psychology, chemistry, and economics and the 10-book *"reader" courses*, such as English literature and history in the same order as your "to-do" list. All of the course materials should be easy to locate. Use a folder filing system for handouts, project outlines, term paper descriptions, articles, and other paperwork. Try plastic buckets from The Container Store if you don't have the space for file cabinets. Use your tickler files for notes, articles, and other stuff that doesn't seem to fit anywhere neatly (see #23).

Collect your books, other course materials, and laptop and put them in your backpack so they're ready to go. Try not to rely on grabbing the right materials at the last minute when you leave your room. Make sure you have what you need for your classes as well as the assignments you can attack while waiting in line for Ludacris or 50 Cent concert tickets that morning.

As the semester progresses and paper products multiply, set up additional file folders as necessary. Remember to use your "to-do" list to guide your course organization so the right materials get into the right places at the right times.

33. Keep a Clean Desk

Now, I know I've stepped over the line by invading your personal work space. But can you see the top of your desk? Wait, let me reword that: Can you see any surface area resembling the wood or fiberboard composition of your desk? Yeah. Me too. You should be ashamed of yourself. Hang your head in shame. Wait, I spotted a corner of your desk. What a mess!! Where did all of the clutter come from? How can you find anything? Where's your PC? Buried under all of this stuff? Sound familiar? I bet you answer: "Don't touch anything. I know exactly where everything is located." Sure you do. RIIIIIGHT!

Studying requires total attention and concentration. Unfortunately, anything on your desk except the materials needed to complete the current assignment can distract you from the task at hand. I know what you're thinking: "Where's my salami sandwich?" No. "I don't have the TIME to clean my desk." Ah-ha. We're back to time again. Schedule the clean-up in your "to-do" list ASAP. It may require several time slots. Wait, let me reword that—It may take hundreds of time slots over many years. In fact, you might still be doing it while finishing your PhD. In other words, you don't have to do it all at once. As the 20-year-old slogan for Nike® says, "Just Do It!" You won't regret it.

If possible, pleeeeeaaase, before you begin the next major study session, remove the following items to clear some space for your PC and keyboard: extra books, Verizon® phone and computer bills, grocery lists, overdue parking tickets, legal papers naming you the guardian of four kids, MapQuests® to various parties, pictures from your trip to South Africa, a brown hairy salami sandwich under term paper drafts from three weeks ago, a pizza box with two slices of petrified pepperoni pizza inside, a Starbucks® coffee cup with mocha green slime growing moss, the aquarium with three dead fish, your ski boots, and your underwear with rigor (mortis), which can stand up by itself and maybe even walk. Now you're ready to study. You probably need only your PC, psych book, Hi-Liter®, and a pencil or pen. Admit it. Don't you feel much better working in a "cleaner" area? "Yeah, but what about those four kids?"

34. Regularly Maintain All Electronic Equipment

If you are as dependent on electronic equipment as I think you are, make sure you maintain all of your equipment. You don't have to be a hardware expert. I'm talking about batteries and portable hard drives. Here are a few ideas to keep you and your equipment fully charged to tackle your daily "to-do" list:

1. Keep lots of AA and AAA alkaline batteries on hand. If you can spring for the cost of lithium batteries, get them instead. You'll need them for your mouse and remotes.
2. Keep specialized replacement batteries on hand for your iPod or MP3 player so you're ready to be entertained when you reach that time slot in your "to-do" list.
3. Recharge all rechargeable batteries in your PDA, iPhone, BlackBerry®, and PC or Mac, plus back-up batteries.
4. Obtain an external drive of 250–500 GB for under $99. This could be your most important investment for your PC or Mac. In case any malfunction occurs with your desktop or laptop, saving all of your work on an independent drive can bail you out. Make sure to save all your work on your back-up drive at the end of every day.
5. Download your PDA schedules onto your PC as frequently as possible (at least once a week) to provide a back-up for your schedules. If you drop your PDA in the fish tank, say "Bye-bye, schedule; hello, titanium paperweight."
6. Track down a knowledgeable, inexpensive computer geek or two who can repair your PC when there is a problem. They usually hang out in the computer sciences department. Don't wait until there's a problem to find a geek.

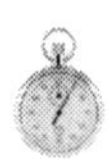

35. Reduce Your Information Overload

Hiding in a residence hall room won't isolate you from the media bombardment of information and advertisements. They will find you wherever you try to hide. Those media will track you down like Dog the Bounty Hunter. The avenues of attack include traditional sources, such as TV, radio, and snail mail, and electronic sources, such as e-mail, TMs, Facebook, MySpace, LinkedIn, Twitter, PC/Mac, CDs, DVDs, MP3s, iPods, iPhones, and BlackBerrys®. The attacks can be launched in your room or in transit at any time.

Just sifting through the information can suck valuable time out of your schedule that could be better spent on course assignments. You don't have much choice until you cut back on the sources. Here are a few suggestions:

1. Remove your name from print and e-mail lists.
2. Check e-mails no more than three times a day (early morning, lunch, and late evening) and delete irrelevant stuff.
3. Tell friends and family to cut down significantly on social e-mails and TMs during the week unless absolutely critical.
4. Cancel print and online subscriptions not directly pertinent to your life as a student.
5. Cut out articles from magazines and journals, discard the sources, and file the articles (see #23).
6. Watch *The Daily Show* or *The Colbert Report* occasionally.

These strategies can markedly increase your time availability. You need to constantly control the information flow from the preceding media sources. Stay on top of e-mail and TMs, especially. They can easily gobble up your time again.

36. Conduct Effective and Efficient Meetings (for Student Government and Fraternity/ Sorority Leaders)

Meetings have a bad reputation because they can be major time wasters, accomplishing very little, and often deteriorating into just another social event. The reason for that reputation and the negative images associated with meetings is putrid leadership. The reputation is well-earned. It's the leader or chair who is totally responsible. Although the men and women who try to conduct meetings are probably wonderful people from law-abiding families with pit bulls surrounded by barbed wire fences, most of them stink at running a meeting properly.

Given this ubiquitous problem with meetings, right now I want you to take your previous experiences in conducting meetings or just sitting in them and scour them from your memory. Block them out completely. Let's begin with a clean slate.

According to experts in business and time management, there are right and wrong ways to conduct meetings. If you follow the guidelines presented here in your student government, fraternity or sorority, or other committee meetings, the time-management benefits will carry over into your career once you've graduated. The workplace doesn't need another putrid leader. Law firms, corporations, universities, Congress, and the White House are in dire need of competent leaders who can run meetings effectively and efficiently.

Here is the best advice from the experts:

1. ***Start and stop on time***: Punctuality is extremely important! If you're not sure about its importance, jump ahead to #37 and take a peek. DO NOT reward attendees for coming in late by recapping

what they missed. Instead, they should be taken out and horsewhipped in a back room. Kidding. You can use any room you like. If you do not end on time, students will be late to classes, other meetings, or other commitments. It's a matter of respect for everyone present.

2. ***Prepare a detailed agenda with times for each item:*** Provide specific information on each topic and explain how those at the meeting can be prepared to discuss or vote on an issue. Solicit input on the items and topics or issues that members want to have addressed. Place the most important items in the middle of the agenda to allow students to warm up and arrive and recover from their horsewhipping. Attach any documents referred to in the agenda so they can be read in advance. Allow a reasonable amount of time for each item to streamline the meeting.

3. ***Distribute the agenda at least a week in advance of meeting time:*** Send out the agenda to all participating students. Tell them to be familiar with all of the items and support documents. If any student is presenting an item, he or she should be thoroughly prepared and cognizant of the assigned time limits. Make it clear that you will hold all students to their respective time limits to keep the meeting on schedule.

4. ***Enforce the assigned times of each agenda item***: Make sure to appoint a parliamentarian to ensure the meeting flows according to *Robert's Rules.* However, a timekeeper is even more important to make sure everyone sticks to the schedule. This appointee has a key time-management role: Get through the agenda on time or earlier. You and your timekeeper are a team, like Barbie and Ken, Ben and Jerry, Kermit and Miss Piggy, and Mercedes and Benz.

Think of the agenda as a "to-do" list with all **A** items. You must get through every item. Everyone has time limits, even you. Model the use of those limits. Use your discretion about when to cut off or summarize discussion. Stop long-winded students politely, if necessary. If that doesn't work, gag them with the agenda. They really need to be smacked, but don't do it until after the meeting. You and your timekeeper should try to keep pace with the original time slots.

5. ***Don't permit agenda-busting:*** Don't ask for items to be added to the agenda at the beginning of the meeting. The students already had input into developing the agenda. They had their chance. If new, important, and/or urgent items arise during the course of the meeting, they can be tabled until the next meeting, or an ad hoc committee can be created to examine the items and report its findings at a future meeting.

6. ***Invite only those who need to attend:*** Try to restrict your "dream team" total to between 5 and 10. This is the optimum range for reaching consensus and making decisions. Larger groups can impede the process. Additional students can serve as observers. Students not attending can be sent copies of the minutes on a need-to-know basis.

7. ***Hold the meeting only if necessary:*** If the information to be presented can be disseminated to committee members electronically or a decision made without a meeting, cancel the meeting. Meet only when the students have to discuss an issue or engage in interaction that could not be effectively achieved online. Conference calls, Webinars, and online votes can save a lot of live meeting time.

8. ***Schedule meetings when participants don't have classes:*** Survey students' schedules to determine time blocks during which none of

the students have classes. Try to use that time for all meetings during the semester.

9. ***Hold the meeting wherever you can find a room:*** Available rooms in a university are rare finds these days. Space is at a premium. Use your secret, hidden room in your Greek house or go off campus to one of the students' apartments, a coffee house, or a nicely decorated tree house during downtime. Be creative.

10. ***Do not serve food regularly—coffee, yes:*** Snacks and burgers can be distracting and costly. Whip through the business that needs to get done. Then go to Smokey Joe's Burnt Burgers for dinner.

11. ***Engage all students in the meeting:*** All of the students present are there for a reason. They have been elected by their class or organization to carry out certain duties or they have chosen to attend because they want to participate. Draw shy students into the discussion. Ask contentious questions. Play devil's advocate. Find ways to get everyone involved and contributing. It's their meeting. Strive for 100% engagement. You are there to facilitate the proceedings.

12. ***Attain closure on every item:*** Every item should end with a decision based on a vote, be referred to a standing or ad hoc committee, or be tabled until the next meeting. Nothing should be left hanging.

13. ***Give a 10-minute warning before the meeting ends:*** This warning snaps everyone to attention and rivets their eyeballs on the remaining agenda items. Everyone goes into high gear. The last 10 minutes are turbo-charged. Everyone must end this meeting on time together.

14. ***Prepare the minutes and executive summary immediately after adjournment:*** Write up the detailed minutes of the meeting and also an executive summary of the decisions made on every agenda item. The minutes document what was done and who does what next by a given date; the executive summary simply lists the decisions reached for all items.

15. ***Disseminate the minutes and executive summary:*** Send out both documents as drafts to all participants. While the meeting's actions are fresh in everyone's minds, request their input on additions, omissions, and corrections to the minutes and summary. After changes are made, send out a final version to all interested students. Make sure to follow up on the tasks that need to be completed with the students who were responsible. These tasks should cover all actions taken at the meeting.

4

General Time Savers

37. Be Punctual

Do you arrive at your classes, meetings with students and professors, lunch and dinner dates, and doctors' appointments on time, as expected, without exception, without excuses, all the time? If yes, congratulations. I'm proud of you. If no, you should be totally ashamed of yourself. What is wrong with you?

Your punctuality is extremely important. When you are consistently punctual, you put yourself in a position of power. Your punctuality makes the statement: "I respect your time as well as my own. And I want to be a power person like Ironman, Spiderman, The Hulk, or Oprah. I want to be your hero." I think you're getting carried away. This paragraph is about being on time, NOT world domination! Time is valuable and should not be wasted by delays for any reason. When you're punctual, you can demand that of others. As a student government or Greek leader, you start your meetings on time and end them on time.

In contrast, if you are not punctual and make no effort to change that behavior, you have no leverage over others. Arriving late regularly to any appointment says: "I have no respect for your time. It's just not that important." Wasting other students' time is insulting. You need to be smacked. How are you going to follow your "to-do" list if you have no regard for time? Everything recommended in this book hinges on the value of your time and how to make the most of it.

A student who cannot keep appointments may not be trusted to do other things. That behavior calls his or her dependability into question. That's significant. If you can't count on somebody in a clutch situation, there's a serious problem. When she says "I've got your back," who will believe her? You better find someone else to cover your back.

Lack of punctuality can also be linked to integrity. Showing lack of respect for your own time questions your values, priorities, honesty, and moral soundness. Remember those values way back in #1? Here is where they count. All of a sudden, simply being late all the time can blow trust, dependability, and integrity off the list. These attributes are not only critical during your college years as you are maturing, but in a few years after you graduate, they can turn into *career makers or breakers*. If you are habitually late to everything, STOP, examine what you're doing, and correct that behavior before it's too late.

38. Learn to Say "NO"

Your "to-do" list schedule is packed to the gills for the next month. Yet you still accept invitations to attend student government meetings and planning committees, and you try out for the tennis and swim teams. These additions to your list set you up for stress, frustration, and disappointment. Why did you add those commitments? (Also see #7.)

There are at least four possible reasons that you over-commit: (1) you are unrealistic in your estimate of the time needed to complete existing assignments, (2) you have difficulty saying no to activities in which you're interested, despite your previous commitments, (3) you have difficulty saying no to requests by the friends or faculty you want to impress, or (4) you're an idiot.

If your "to-do" list is full, try to assess whether there is any wiggle room to handle other tasks without compromising your work on existing assignments. Be realistic. Leave yourself extra time for completion of big projects and papers in case you're not sure. Considering this schedule, say NO to any tempting invitations. Stick to your prioritized list. If there is an opening on the tennis team this year, there will probably be one next year.

Defer invitations from your friends. Tell them:

- "This is not the best time . . ."
- "I have other priorities right now . . ."
- "I have too much on my plate right now . . ."
- "I could probably get to it in three weeks. Check back with me then."
- "I couldn't possibly do it justice with my current workload."
- "I appreciate your confidence in me, but this is not a good time."
- "I have a paper cut. Sorry."
- "I'm a putrid leader. You don't want me to chair the committee until I've read Berk's book."

- "I'm not very punctual, so my trust, dependability, and integrity are shot."
- "Let me finish my salami sandwich and pickle first. Then I'll think about your request."
- "Are you crazy? I don't even know you."

In order to stay in control of YOUR schedule, you need to say NO to the most attractive activities proffered by your closest friends. If you don't, you will have to deal with the consequences. Do I have to repeat those consequences? I don't think so.

 39. Avoid Peak Times

Standing in line and sitting in traffic are major time wasters, and may be dangerous. (*Note:* See examples of in-transit time wasters in #24 and the list of 20 time wasters in #25.) Whatever errands and tasks you have to complete, make every effort to do them at nonpeak times. If you can avoid the most crowded times for accomplishing your routine errands, you can save a lot of time and prevent the frustration and anger that accompanies wasting time.

For example, if you commute to campus, you already know how to avoid the morning and afternoon rush hours. Apply the same strategy to the nonpeak times when you go to the bank, post office, Laundromat, grocery store, coffee bar, and airport. Check in and out of hotels and schedule airline flights at off times. Avoid "herd behavior." Plan these nonpeak times in advance by choosing the appropriate slots in your "to-do" list. They will become automatic choices in your schedule.

40. Communicate Succinctly and Precisely

What's this book all about? "I forgot." Haven't you been paying attention? "Waste." "Toxic waste?" "No. Wasting time." That's it. Using time wisely. Get to the point. Stop playing around. In all of your communications, be succinct and precise. If you waste words, you waste time. Consider the following:

1. ***e-mail and TM:***
   a. Be brief, focused, and concise, but thorough.
   b. Use normal grammar, punctuation, and spelling unless the reader knows your abbreviations and symbols.
   c. Edit carefully.
   d. If in HTML, use font colors, underlining, boldface, highlight colors, and italics to highlight key points
   e. Identify contents in the Subject field.
   f. Use a signature line with your contact information (phone, e-mail, Web, etc.).
   g. Return messages within 24 hours.
   h. Don't forward jokes, chain letters, ads, or junk to friends without reading or editing contents first.
   i. Don't use offensive language, such as profanity and vulgarity, or off-color pics or graphics.
   j. Don't use e-mail or TM for confidential, complicated, emotional, or high-security messages; instead, handle those situations face to face.

2. ***Voice mail:***
   a. Plan what you're going to say.
   b. Be brief, specific, and (Say it with me) "get to the point."
   c. Enunciate every word; don't mumble, garble, slur, spit, or drool your words.

d. Leave a call-back number; speak slowly and repeat it.
e. Provide times when you will be available to reduce phone tag.
f. If someone answers, say you want to leave a voice mail message.

3. ***Phone calls:***
   a. Outline main points for a complex call, such as reviewing for a test.
   b. Stay focused.
   c. Speak in small bites.
   d. Enunciate every word.
   e. "Get to the point," and tell the caller to do the same.
   f. Return calls within 24 hours.
   g. Prioritize your calls in order of importance and urgency.

41. Get Eight Hours of Sleep

Most of the people in this country are sleep deprived. However, college students have clearly paved the way and taken the lead in this category. "Late nighters" and "all nighters" have always been used by students to play catch-up, study for tests, fool around, and party. They're not new. Students have a long (2,000 years, give or take a month), distinctive, and proud tradition of sleep deprivation. Do you stay up until 3 A.M. every night? You're not alone.

If you're one of these chronically drowsy, but proud, late-nighter types, wouldn't it be nice if you could sleep it off the next day? Depending on your schedule, that might be possible sometimes, but not always. Contrary to what you might think, highly motivated students can overcome the negative effects of sleep loss by trying harder, which can significantly improve performance. This compensatory behavior, however, is successful only up to a point.

Occasional and cumulative sleep loss can have a pronounced effect on academic performance. A dearth of sleep can impair your cognitive function and ability to concentrate and make decisions. You can end up dozing off in class or nodding off while reading text material, studying for a test, or solving problems that are really borrrrring. Consider the image of sleeping and drooling on whatever you're doing. When you look in the mirror and see someone who resembles one of the zombies in Michael Jackson's "Thriller," you're in BIIIIG trouble. Zombies do not function effectively with boring, deadly course content. You need to be at peak level to reach high productivity for that type of content. Listen to your body. When it says "SLEEEEEEEEP, knucklehead," pay attention or your zombie self will end up in Neverland.

Physiologically, the picture gets worse. Sleep deprivation can decrease your motor skills performance, such as response time while driving, and your neurological and immune system functions that fight off infection and disease. Insufficient sleep has also been linked to the onset and aggravation of several chronic conditions, such as diabetes, cardiovascular disease, obesity, and depression. Mega-doses of caffeine or other stimulants or neuroenhancers such as Adderall®, Ritalin®, or Concerta® may provide a temporary solution to keep you functioning, but they won't prevent the aforementioned conditions. In addition, the neuroenhancers have serious, life-threatening side effects. They cannot replace your body's need for sleep.

So how can you change your sleep habits? The recommendations of the Centers for Disease Control (CDC) are probably contrary to most of your current practices. Here they are:

1. Remove TVs, PCs, and other technological gadgets from your room.
2. Avoid taking paperwork, your laptop, or anything inflatable into bed with you.
3. Avoid large meals, such as pizza and beer, lasagna with garlic bread, or a BIG, THICK salami sandwich with pickles, before bedtime (this list is making me hungry, agaaain). (*Note:* This food can also give you Freddy Kreuger-type nightmares once you fall asleep.)
4. Avoid caffeinated beverages after *lunch.*
5. Avoid strenuous exercise or activity for two to three hours before bedtime.
6. Avoid bright light in your room in the evening.
7. Avoid stimulating activities, such as studying, TMs, long conversations, a Leonardo Di Caprio, Matt Damon, Penélope Cruz, or Halle Berry flick, or any *CSI* or *Law & Order* episode, near bedtime.
8. Avoid "all-nighters."

I know what you're thinking: "ARE YOU NUTS?" or "JUST KILL ME NOW!" I bet you can definitely nail number 6. The others may take a little time to conquer, but don't give up yet. You can do it. Take them one at a time. Record them in your "not-to-do" list. They will become routine just like the rest of your list. Alternatively, consider #42.

42. Take a Nap if You Feel Exhausted

If you're sitting at your PC screen, reading Toni Morrison, or slogging through the pages of a history text, and your eyelids keep closing, then you start nodding off, HELLLO!! Your body is telling you something—IT DOESN'T WANT TO GO TO NEVERLAND. That's a "bad" place. It NEEDS SLEEP because it wants to be in an MJ video. In fact, reading these sentences is making me sleepy. Take a nap for an hour or two. Longer naps can throw off your regular sleep schedule. Make sure to set your alarm correctly or tell your dependable roommate to wake you at a specific time. Then you will pop up and get back to work.

When you're that tired, for whatever reason (don't tell me; I don't want to know), you can't focus or absorb anything. So why bother studying? Get some rest so you will be refreshed, like the refresh icon at the top of your Windows Explorer screen. After the nap, tackle one of the more challenging assignments first. That will wake you up and create an adrenalin rush. Then move on to the easier ones. The next time you have the opportunity for a full night's sleep, take it, or else—you know where you could end up.

43. Eat Properly

Eventually you're going to get sick and tired of pizza and beer and order sushi or kung pao chicken. And those Ho Hos® and Doritos® won't help much either. You're going to have to consider real food at some point. Right now I bet you're thinking: "You've just put me in the mood for Ho Hos®. So what does my food have to do with time management?" Aha! Thanks for putting me back on track.

There is a strong link between food and mood, performance, and brain function. If you eat the wrong foods, you will probably operate like an inefficient and ineffective slug at completing your coursework. However, if you decide to eat the right foods at the right times in the right amounts, you could be operating like a turbo-charged, efficient, and effective slug. That's like a ginormous difference, dude (or dudette).

For ***peak performance and high productivity***, eat foods *high in protein and low in fat and carbs.* These foods will increase your mental alertness, quickness, energy, and attention. For ***relaxation and concentration***, eat foods *high in sugar and starch and low in protein and fat.* No wonder you're so relaxed all the time. Junk food is your secret.

BERK'S BOTTOM LINE: Your best strategies to get through most of the **A**s in your "to-do" list are to *eat a high-protein breakfast and work intensively from 6 A.M. to noon*, which is when your mental and physical energy levels are at their peak (also see #16). Of course, you will probably be weaving in and out of classes during that time. As the day progresses, your energy levels gradually decline. If you want to have a highly productive evening, eat a high-protein dinner. In other words, to whip through your "to-do" list, you will be consuming truckloads of eggs, chicken, fish, veal, lean beef, lentils, and tofu. If you want to funk out, stick with your pizza, Ho Hos®, and other desserts. It's your choice.

44. Exercise Regularly

Your archery or bowling class doesn't provide enough exercise, but then you knew that. Exergames, such as Nintendo's *Wii Fit*, may also be inadequate. Who has time for exercise? You will if you follow the techniques in this book. There is a positive relationship between regular exercise (the operative word here is *regular*) and improved mental functioning, performance, attitudes, feelings, moods, and self-esteem. These effects result from at least 15 to 20 minutes of aerobic exercise, three times a week.

The big payoff aerobic activities include walking, running, biking, swimming, snowboarding, cross-country (Nordic) skiing, bronco riding, bull fighting, car waxing, house roofing, and mud wrestling. Engaging in any one or a combination of those activities before breakfast or before dinner can really charge your batteries to conquer those **A**s and **B**s. Mark my words, there's nothing that can jumpstart your day like a good mud wrestle.

45. "If It Doesn't Get Done, It Just Wasn't Important Enough!"

When the day is over, the dust has settled, and you're ready to ride off into the sunset on your bike to create new dust, like Ole Snoop Lil' Dog Diggy Puff, all of a sudden you realize you didn't finish a particular **A** task in your list. There is usually just one explanation: You spilled your café mocha on your "to-do" list and couldn't read the task. You wish! Rather, it just wasn't important enough.

It's that simple. It all hinges on priorities. Those words—"*It just wasn't important enough*"—were uttered by my wife 30 years ago when I returned from the library one day complaining that I didn't finish writing the journal article I had planned to complete. The words just stuck in my brain. I examined the reasons the article didn't get done. Since then, that quote has served as a criterion that I apply consciously or unconsciously to every article, chapter, book, and class preparation, plus other academic activities and personal commitments.

Those words also apply to everything *YOU* do. This is the second mantra of this book. The first was stated in the Introduction. Remember it? "*Get to the Point—Don't Waste My Time!*" To that one you can now add "*If It Doesn't Get Done, It Just Wasn't Important Enough!*"

Those two mantras should reverberate in your noggin as you're working on any project. If it's important and must be completed by a deadline (urgent), get to the point, push everything else aside, eliminate distractions, remove temptations, say no to anything that can derail what you're doing, and TOTALLY FOCUS on the task at hand. Don't let anything pull that focus until the job is done. That's effective and efficient time management.

Epilogue

THIS BOOK IS NOW COMPLETE. YOU HAVE "THE ALPHA AND the omega," "the yin and the yang," "the hither and the yon," "the to and the fro," and "the Click and the Clack." You are armed with state-of-the-art techniques in time management, unless, of course, you skipped over some of the sections. May you have buckets of time to accomplish all of your college and life goals.

QUICK ORDER FORM

(copy this form)

Fax orders: 1-888-401-8089. Send a copy of this form.

Telephone orders: 1-410-730-9339. Have your credit card ready.

Email orders: rberk@son.jhmi.edu

Postal orders: Coventry Press
10971 Swansfield Rd.
Columbia, MD 21044

Please send ______ copies (fewer than 15) of *The Five-Minute Time Manager for College Students* at $16.95 each

Sales tax: Please add 6% for Maryland addresses.

Shipping cost: $6.95 for first copy, $3.00 for each additional copy

Checks payable to: Coventry Press

Quantity discounts: See next page or www.coventrypress.com

SEND BOOK(S) TO:

Name: ____

Address: ____

City: ___________________________ **State:** ____ **Zip:** _________

Phone: ____________________ **Email:** ____________________

Credit card: __VISA __MasterCard **Exp. Date:** ________

Card Number: ____

CSC (3-digit no.) ______ **Name on card:** ____________________

Signature: ___________________________ **Date:** ___________

SEND ME FREE INFORMATION ON THE FOLLOWING:

____ Speaking ____Consulting ____Other Books & Products

QUANTITY DISCOUNTS

IF YOU HAVE BOOKED RON BERK TO SPEAK AT YOUR INSTITUTION, YOU ARE ENTITLED TO RECEIVE SPECIAL DISCOUNTED PRICES ON:

***The Five-Minute Time Manager for College Students* (2009)**

(List price = $16.95) (*Note:* Shipping costs extra.)

QUANTITY	COST PER BOOK	TOTAL
15–29	$15.00	$225 +
30–59	$14.00	$420 +
60–99	$13.00	$780 +
100–299	$12.00	$1200 +
300 +	$10.00	$3000 +

SIX Reasons to Pre-Order Books

1. ***INCREASE ATTENDANCE*** by advertising that everyone (or the first ____ who register) will receive a FREE book. If conference fee is several hundred dollars and at least 100 people attend, a $10 or $12 add-on is insignificant.
2. ***REWARD STUDENTS*** for something special they did or for outstanding performance.
3. ***USE AS DOOR PRIZES*** and benefit from the lower prices.
4. ***ANNOUNCE A BOOK SIGNING*** in advance to increase attendance and give people a lower rate.
5. ***RECEIVE THE DISCOUNTED PRICE,*** which is lower than the normal book signing discount.
6. ***RAISE MONEY FOR YOUR INSTITUTION*** by buying books at the discounted price and selling them at the event for a slight mark-up.

- -

I am interested in ordering ____________________ (Qty.) copies of *The Five-Minute Time Manager*

Name (print or type) ________________________________

Signature ______________________________________

Fax order: 1-888-410-8089 **OR Call:** 1-410-730-9339

CPSIA information can be obtained at www.ICGtesting.com
Printed in the USA
BVOW070327130712

295092BV00001B/60/P